Acadian Root Baskets
of Atlantic Canada

Joleen Gordon

NIMBUS
PUBLISHING LTD

AND THE NOVA SCOTIA MUSEUM

Crown Copyright © Province of Nova Scotia, 2005

All rights reserved. No part of this book may be reproduced, stored in a retrieval system or transmitted in any form or by any means without the prior written permission from the publisher, or, in the case of photocopying or other reprographic copying, permission from Access Copyright, 1 Yonge Street, Suite 1900, Toronto, Ontario M5E 1E5.

Nimbus Publishing Limited
PO Box 9166
Halifax, NS   B3K 5M8
(902) 455-4286

Printed and bound in Canada

Editors: Ruth Holmes Whitehead and Scott Robson
Design: Kathy Kaulbach, Paragon Design Group

Front Cover image: Michele Gallant
Back Cover / Title Page: Detail of ribbed basket in "Le Départ vers l'Exil, 1755." Claude T. Picard. 1986. Painted in the series "Deportation of the Acadians" for Grand Pré National Historic Site, Nova Scotia. The artist is from Saint-Basile, New Brunswick. Parks Canada, Halifax, H-03-08-01-00(04).

Library and Archives Canada Cataloguing in Publication

> Gordon, Joleen
> Acadian root baskets of Atlantic Canada / Joleen Gordon.
> ISBN 1-55109-524-6

1. Basket making—Atlantic Provinces. 2. Basket makers—Atlantic Provinces. 3. Acadians. 4. Basket making. I. Title.
TT879.B3G67 2005   746.41'2'0891140715   C2005-902676-6

We acknowledge the financial support of the Government of Canada through the Book Publishing Industry Development Program (BPIDP) and the Canada Council, and of the Province of Nova Scotia through the Department of Tourism, Culture and Heritage for our publishing activities.

Table of Contents

Glossary iv

Introduction 1
Root: Mother Nature's Thread. 4
The Ribbed Basket 8
    The Ribbed Basket in the Old World 10
    The Ribbed Basket in the New World 14
Root Baskets of Nova Scotia 18
    The Baskets of George Saulnier 29
Root Baskets of New Brunswick 31
    The Baskets of Lazare Duguay 33
Root Baskets of Newfoundland 36
    The Baskets of Anthony White 44
Making an Acadian Root Basket Step-by-Step . . . 50
    STEP 1 ■ Gathering and Preparing Root Materials . 51
    STEP 2 ■ Gathering and Preparing Wood Materials 54
    STEP 3 ■ Constructing the Framework 56
    STEP 4 ■ Creating the Ears / les Oreilles 58
    STEP 5 ■ Stabilizing the Framework 60
    STEP 6 ■ Preparing and Adding the Ribs 61
    STEP 7 ■ Weaving the Basket 63
    STEP 8 ■ Wrapping the Handle 66
    STEP 9 ■ Drying and Using 68
Conclusion 69

Appendix One: Resource List 73
Notes 74
Acknowledgements 77
Bibliography 82

Glossary

Cane: commercial basketry material derived from the vine *Calamus*, which grows in Southeast Asia and China. The thorny outer bark is discarded; the shiny inner bark is machine-cut into various widths for use in chair-seat caning and basketmaking; the inner pith is machine-cut into various sizes of round and flat material called reed.

Crooked knife: type of knife associated with the Mi'kmaq, Maliseet and others. The blade, usually made of a reworked steel file, is set into a curved handle, against which the thumb is braced. Such knives are pulled toward the user, as a draw-knife.

Kinking: to bend a rod of willow. Kinks cannot be removed, so they are to be avoided unless desired.

Rib: an element of the framework of a ribbed basket. Ribs are made from woodland shoots or carved pieces of wood, either end of which is shaved to a point and set into the wrap that joins the handle and rim circles together.

Rinding out: the process of removing the rind or bark.

Rod: a flexible shoot of woodland shrub suitable for weaving.

Roping: a process of twisting a woodland shoot, enabling it to be smoothly woven or bent without kinking.

Standard: the warp, or upright "standing" element of a basket, around which the weft is woven.

Treen-pegged: a join made with a wooden peg inserted into holes drilled into two pieces of wood, or of wood and of bark.

Turnback: the movement of turning a weaver back on a rib rather than weaving it for the full row and turning it around the rim. Turnbacks are used to fill in areas on either side of a basket, making the two lines of weaving on either side of the basket parallel, so the weaving will come together along the centre line of the basket.

Weaver: a piece of material, root, withe, stick, or rod used as a weft; also, a person who weaves. Most of the time this distinction is evident, other times it can be amusingly confusing.

Weft: the element of a basket that is woven around a framework of ribs or standards.

Withe, Wit, Willie: a flexible shoot of woodland shrubbery.

Witherod: a flexible shoot of a specific woodland shrub, *Viburnum cassinoides*, also known in Nova Scotia as Indian wits or wild raisin.

Wrap: The method of joining the handle and rim circle of a basket together. It may take the form of an X with four small pockets for rib insertion; a larger 3-point wrap with four larger pockets for the ribs; or a 4-point diamond-shaped wrap where there are no pockets, with the ribs set between the back sides of the wraps on either side of the basket, and held there by tension.

FIGURE 1
Atlantic region of Canada showing locations of basketmaking communitites mentioned in this book.

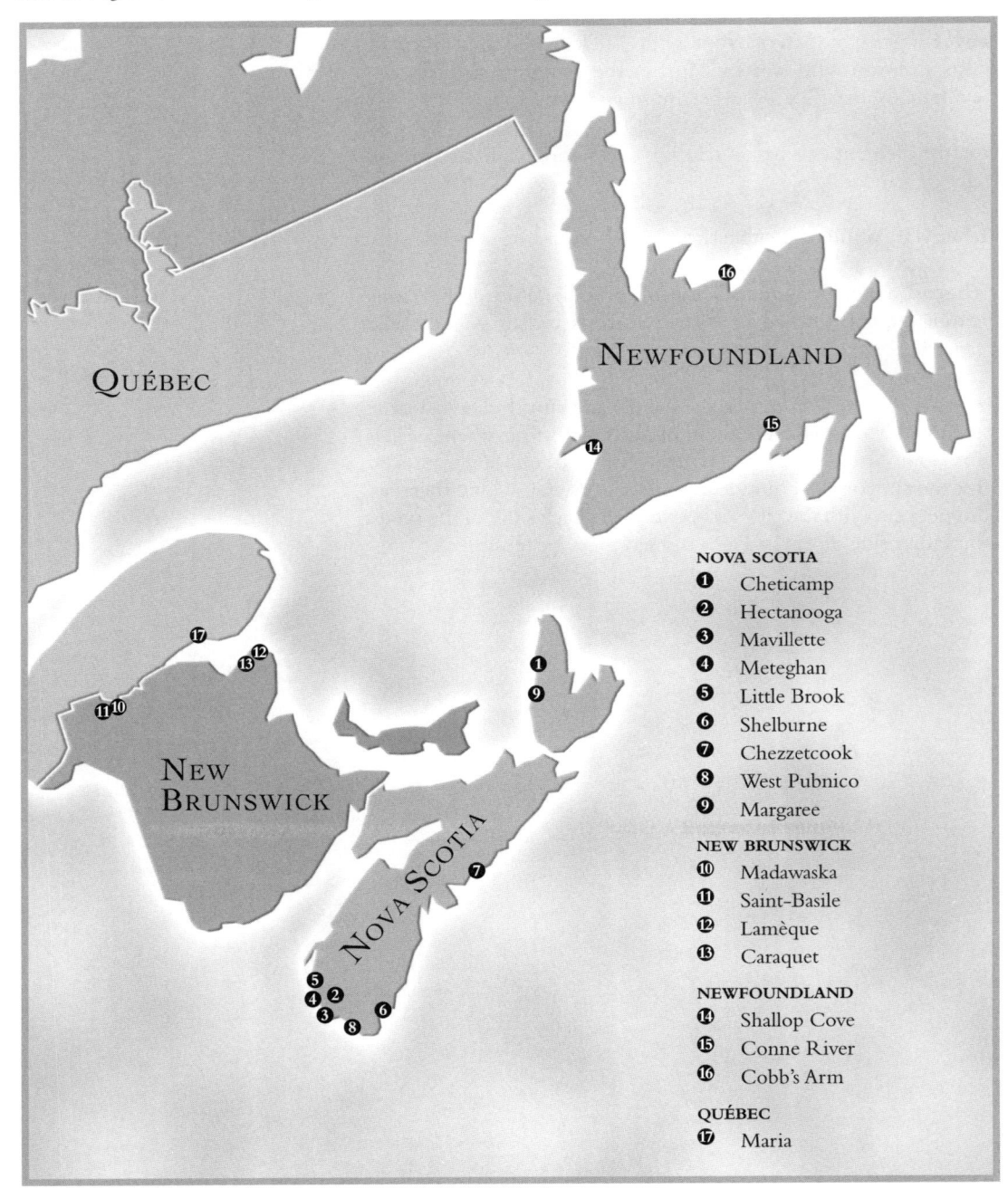

NOVA SCOTIA
1. Cheticamp
2. Hectanooga
3. Mavillette
4. Meteghan
5. Little Brook
6. Shelburne
7. Chezzetcook
8. West Pubnico
9. Margaree

NEW BRUNSWICK
10. Madawaska
11. Saint-Basile
12. Lamèque
13. Caraquet

NEWFOUNDLAND
14. Shallop Cove
15. Conne River
16. Cobb's Arm

QUÉBEC
17. Maria

Introduction

EVERY BASKET MADE BY HAND holds a story—a story of its maker and how he or she learned the craft, of its materials and the season in which they were collected, and of its era and how the basket was constructed. It is also a story of the intended use of the basket and its role in the life and economy of the community.

Atlantic Canada has a rich heritage of basketmaking. (FIGURE 1) For many generations, Mi'kmaq and Maliseet First Nations people have experimented with plant and animal materials to weave baskets and matting. Perhaps the earliest known basketry in this region, almost twenty-five hundred years old, comes from fragments found in the Augustine Mound site in Red Bank, New Brunswick, in which cattail leaves, cedar bark strips, porcupine quills and hairs, animal sinew, and leather were worked with twining and plaiting techniques. Late-1500s archaeological sites in Nova Scotia and New Brunswick reveal the Mi'kmaq used not only cattail leaves and cedar bark, but also rushes and grasses in plaiting, twining, twilling, and sewing techniques. Their knowledge of what was available, when to gather it, and how to work with it was unparalleled[1]. Today, the Mi'kmaq and Maliseet weave both sturdy and fancy baskets from thin, ribbon-like splints of ash, maple, and poplar wood, some colourfully dyed, embossed with projecting splints, or decorated with fragrant strands of sweetgrass. Mi'kmaq weavers living in Maria, Québec, make a ribbed basket of ash wood. Other containers, made of cut and folded birchbark, are stitched together with spruce root[2]. Their work is sold from their homes, in First Nations shops, and at some tourist sites in the province.

Beginning in the early 1600s, there were several waves of immigration from Europe as people sought a fresh start in the New World. Settlers from France, Scotland, England, Ireland, and Germany brought their traditions, which included basketry. The first permanent European settlers, the French Acadians, were known to have used two styles of baskets: an oval-shaped basket to be slung over the shoulder on a rope for sowing seeds, and a huge fan-shaped basket for winnowing grain. There is scant written documentation of Acadian basketry[3].

Fishermen of European descent living on both the eastern and southern shores of Nova Scotia wove cone-shaped eel traps, or eel pots, as well as large baskets for use on fishing schooners. Their descendants continue these weaving traditions, making garden baskets of woodland withies such as witherod or willow. These baskets are woven primarily by men in Lunenburg and Halifax counties and are sold directly to the customer, although one or two men produce on a larger scale for retail shops[4].

Soon after the War of 1812, disbanded soldiers of English and Irish origin were granted land in the New Ross area of Lunenburg County, Nova Scotia. Their wives brought the skill of making braided straw and braided wood hats and baskets, which they passed to the present generation through oral history. Although the craft is not for sale anywhere in the province today, it is part of the craft demonstration program of the Ross Farm Museum[5].

Members of the Black community in the Halifax-Dartmouth area have been weaving ribbed baskets of red maple ever since they arrived soon after the War of 1812. Generally in this community, the men cut the wood and the women weave the baskets, although a few men have woven as well. These baskets continue to be offered for sale at the Saturday morning Halifax Farmers' Market, a tradition dating from the mid-nineteenth century[6].

Despite intermingling of cultures, each group of basketmakers has maintained its own basket style woven with specific materials. Within each cultural group, there may be subtle differences due to the personal preference of the basketmaker, such as rib placement, weaver addition, and shape experimentation. This differentation of style grows out of pride in their work and respect for other basketmakers. For example, within the Acadian community, artisans buy Mi'kmaq baskets rather than replicate them. They still have great respect for the Mi'kmaq for helping the early Acadians survive off the land.

This is a study of the basketry of the Acadian people living in Atlantic Canada. Taped oral history interviews and written family records show that several generations of Acadians living in western Newfoundland, northern New Brunswick, and along the Digby County shore of Nova Scotia (also known as the French Shore) have been making a distinctive style of ribbed basket woven with peeled and split roots. Within recent memory, there were several men in each of these areas weaving a distinctive style of root-woven ribbed basket for themselves and their neighbours. Unfortunately, many of them have passed away and the craft has died in their communities. This book is an attempt to capture this craft, recognize past artists, and encourage future basketmakers for generations to come.

This story of the Acadian root-woven ribbed basket begins with the weaving material, tree root, and its use in the material culture of Atlantic Canadians. This is followed by a discussion of the ribbed-basket design, its origins in Europe, and how it came to North America. Then, the root-woven ribbed baskets found in each region of Atlantic Canada are described separately; this is out of respect for the weavers who worked in isolation, each developing a unique approach. Finally, there is a detailed step-by-step documentation of George Saulnier of Hectanooga, Nova Scotia, making one of his baskets.

Root: Mother Nature's Thread

ROOTS ARE A NATURAL thread-like material. They are long, supple, strong, and durable, making them suitable for wrapping, binding, stitching, and weaving. Easily gathered by digging in soil near any woody shrub or tree, they can be collected any time of year the ground is not frozen. For centuries, people living in the northern regions of Canada, the United States, Russia, China, Norway, Sweden, and Finland have made root containers using roots of willow, spruce, birch and tamarack depending on their availability, pliability, and resin content. Many of these skills are alive today in the hands of people making baskets in one of two ways: either solely with root, or with another material like tree bark[7].

Perhaps the oldest basket in Canada made entirely of root was discovered in 1980 at the southern end of Brooman Point, on the east coast of Bathurst Island in the Canadian Arctic. (FIGURE 2) Measuring six centimetres, this small, sac-shaped basket was made with a coiling technique which wraps and stitches finely split roots around a core of whole root. The container was discovered in an archaeological site of mixed Dorset and Thule culture, dated 1200 A.D. Because it was frozen above ground, it survived the cold Arctic in pristine condition. The function of the basket is unknown, but at the time of its discovery it held a number of small Dorset carvings. It is the only known complete example, although fragments of coiled baskets have been found in Norse sites in Greenland[8].

Similarly, the oldest root-sewn bark container found in Canada is also of Norse provenance. Excavation of the Norse site at L'Anse aux Meadows in northern Newfoundland revealed a small cylinder of birchbark (from *Betula papyrifera*)

FIGURE 2
Coiled root basket, 6 x 5 x 2.5 cm, found at an archaeological site at Brooman Point, Bathurst Island.
Canadian Museum of Civilization, Gatineau. 82002-5333.

held together with a root-sewn seam (FIGURE 3). The container was made by overlapping two ends of a piece of bark, adding a length of root on top of the overlap to reinforce the seam, and stitching over both the seam and the root with horizontal stitches. The Norse people of that time, about 1000 A.D., were known to have used such containers, filled with stones, as weights on their fishing nets to stretch out the mesh. Archaeologists also found several pieces of twined rope made of fine spruce roots, plus a bundle of neatly coiled thicker spruce roots near a boat shed at the same site. It is known that the Norse people of that time used fine roots for lashing planking to boat ribs[9].

The early First Nations people living in Atlantic Canada—the Beothuk, the Mi'kmaq, and the Maliseet—used root cordage to lash together their wooden wigwam frames. Worked wet, it dries to an unmovable hardness. As a sewing thread, it can be split to any thickness, as well as dyed or painted. All three groups of people created a wide variety of birchbark containers sewn with spruce root, including their large ocean-going canoes. The Beothuk, in addition, used roots to decorate sewn birchbark containers[10]. A large oval container, rubbed with red ochre, was found in the 1820s in the Red Indian Lake, NL, burial site. It has a narrow collar of bark, cut with a sawtoothed edge, added to the top of the bark container and decorated with elaborate root stitching; the rim is reinforced with a root-wrapped piece of wood. (FIGURE 4)

FIGURE 3
Fragment of a birch bark container, 8.5 x 4 x 4 cm, sewn with root from L'Anse aux Meadows, Newfoundland.
Photo: G. Vandervloogt. Parks Canada, Halifax. 4A70F1-1; RA 2471B.

FIGURE 4
Beothuk birchbark container, 46 x 15cm wide x 19 cm, from Red Indian Lake, Newfoundland.
British Museum. 6975 - PS 023174.

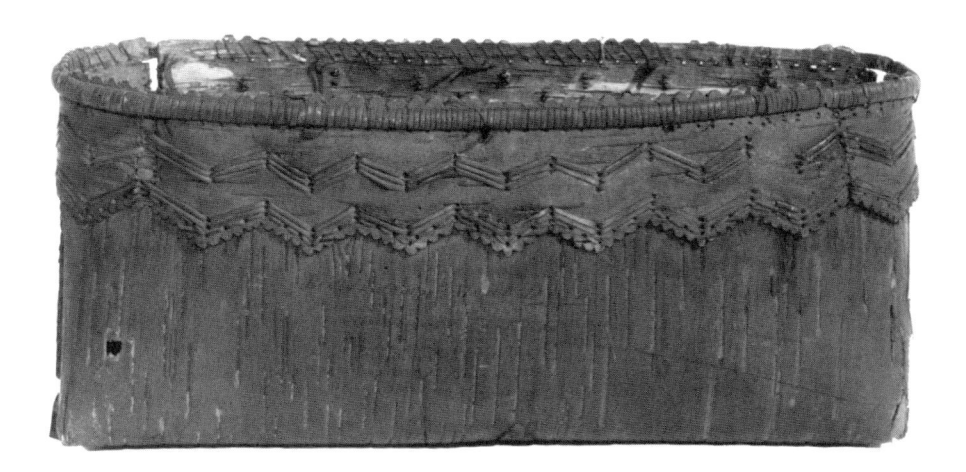

FIGURE 5 [right]
Mi'kmaq birchbark container, 23 x 17 x 7.5 cm, sewn with root. Found in a well at Fortress Louisbourg, Cape Breton Island. Photo: V. McComber. Parks Canada, National Historic Sites. Cat. no. 2L27R6.1: neg. no. x69-681.

FIGURE 6 [below]
Mi'kmaq birchbark and root container, 5.9 x 8 x 8 cm. Maker and date unknown. Photo: Scott Robson. Nova Scotia Museum, History Collection, Halifax. 69.95.2.

In 1606, Parisian lawyer Marc Lescarbot travelled to Acadie (now Nova Scotia) where he spent a year with the Mi'kmaq. His memoirs describe how the Mi'kmaq of that time made bark dishes sewn with roots: "They made their dishes, large and small, of bark. They sewed them with the Fir roots so well that they held water. They ornamented some of them with quills of Porcupine"[11].

The earliest known surviving Mi'kmaq root-sewn birchbark container was found in a well in the French fortress of Louisbourg on Cape Breton Island, Nova Scotia. It has been dated 1723–1784. The tall, conical shape of the container suggests that it was used for food storage. Side seams have been reinforced with an overlying strip of root, similar to the Norse fishing net sinker described earlier, while a wooden rim has been lashed on with root (FIGURE 5).

The Mi'kmaq also made birchbark containers with sides formed by slipping root-wrapped bark rings over a bark liner, which was either root-stitched to a bark base or treen-pegged to a wood base. The bark lids, formed in the same way, were covered with geometric patterns of dyed porcupine quills (FIGURE 6). These bark containers have been well documented by Ruth Holmes Whitehead in *Micmac Quillwork*.

In the folklore of many First Nations people, roots are mentioned in stories of basketry origin. Peter Ginnish, a Mi'kmaq of Burnt Church, New Brunswick, told the following story in 1912:

> A lazy woman was lying down. She rose, scratched the ground, and found a long root. She split it at one end with her teeth; then holding one end in her teeth, and grasping the other end with her hand, split it lengthwise, into two long fibers. She removed the bark. She did the same with another root. She wrapped the root around her fingers several times, leaving eight strands sticking out. The eight pieces served as eight ribs, the warp around which she wove another root, running it alternately in and out of the ribs until the basket was finished. This she showed to the people. No one could name it. It was the first time one had been made, and no one knew what to call it. Next day, the people came to see the thing she had made. They noticed that the bottom of the basket was round, and that the ribs had been filled to the top. They thought it queer; for they had never seen anything like it....The woman made a little handle, and the basket was finished.[12]

The Ribbed Basket

THE MOST COMMON FORM of ribbed basket is the gathering basket with a single, overhand handle in which two hoops are held together at right angles at their point of intersection by a wrap. The less common form has no handle. In the gathering basket, the horizontal hoop becomes the rim of the basket, and the vertical hoop forms the handle and bottom rib. The rim hoop is usually set inside the handle hoop, but there are exceptions.

The wrap varies from a simple X shape to a larger 3-point wrap, and to an even larger 4-point diamond-shaped wrap. Most baskets in this book are made with the diamond wrap. The wrap and the weaving are done with a variety of materials, depending on what is available—roots, vines, whole twigs, or split wood. Ribs of carved wood or whole shoots are either inserted into the pockets created by the simple X and 3-point wrap, or braced between the inside surfaces of the diamond wrap. The ribs give the basket its shape, and its framework.

Weaving is done from either side, beginning near each wrap and going around each rib consecutively in an over-one/under-one pattern. When the weaving reaches the rim, the material is turned around the rim once or twice before beginning the next row. Weaving alternates from each side towards the middle, with the last row woven along the midline of the basket. In some basket shapes, turnbacks are needed to ensure the weaving is parallel at the midline. A turnback is made by turning the material back around the same ribs on each side of the basket, producing incomplete rows of weaving. This has the effect of filling in areas with extra weaving.

Defining ribbed-basket construction may seem to be fairly simple. This is, however, not the case. A single basketmaker may produce many different shapes and sizes in a lifetime, each form presenting its own challenges to the weaver, let alone to the researcher wishing to describe a generic technique.

A framework made of two circular hoops of the same size that intersect at their midpoints, so that the lengths of each half-hoop are equal, means that either hoop could become the handle, while still producing the same size and shape of basket. Such a framework needs only one set of ribs to make a round melon shape. It does not require weaving turnbacks, because the two sides of weaving come together in the midline of the basket.

A framework made of two oval hoops presents two possibilities. Two oval hoops of the same size may be intersected at midpoints along their long axes (with the two wraps far apart), producing a balanced framework requiring one set of ribs and no turnbacks. If, on the other hand, the two oval hoops are intersected at their midpoints on the short axis (with the two wraps closer), the framework is a deep and narrow basket with a high handle. In such a framework, the length of the bottom rib is much longer than the rims on either side. This means that more than a single set of ribs is required as the weaving progresses outward from the wrap, and several sets of turnbacks are needed to make the two rows of weaving parallel.

Some basketmakers use moulds to make their basket hoops the same size, but more often they are made by eye. A combination of one round and one oval hoop intersecting below their midpoints produces the familiar market basket with the high handle requiring several sets of ribs and turnbacks; a labour-intensive project. As George Saulnier has said, "There's a lot of work to make a basket."[13]

The hamper style of ribbed basket has no overhand handle. The rim is a round or oval hoop and the bottom rib is a half hoop, the projecting ends of which are nailed to the rim on either side. This intersection is bound with peeled and split root in a simple X, 3-point, or 4-point wrap. The framework of ribs is added and woven in much the same way as the gathering basket. Sometimes, two "hand-hold" handles are created on the sides away from the wraps by turning the weaver back on the rib just below the rim so that the exposed rim becomes a handle.

In making both the gathering basket and the hamper, there are several ways of adding new weaving material. Thin, flexible material may be knotted together. Thicker material may be sharpened and inserted alongside a rib and then laid horizontally in the weaving; overlapped and woven together with the old weaver for a short distance; or, the old and the new weavers may meet behind one rib.

The Ribbed Basket in the Old World

THE MANY POSSIBILITIES innate in ribbed-basketry technique perhaps explain why there are so many kinds of ribbed baskets in the world. Ribbed baskets have been associated with the working people of Great Britain and continental Europe. Dorothy Wright, a British basket historian, believed this style of basket was made well before the rise of strict professional guilds in Britain. "Frame or ribbed baskets are probably one of the oldest types in Britain and were seldom, if ever, made by professional basketmakers. Fishermen, farmers and other country people made them for their own use"[14]. Itinerant workers also made ribbed baskets, known as "gypsy baskets," for sale to farmers and gardeners. Ribbed baskets were also made in France, where basket historians R. Duchesne, H. Ferrand, and J. Thomas acknowledged that they were in a different category from all other baskets, calling them "*très ancienne and vannerie rustique*"[15].

No one knows exactly when and where the first ribbed basket was made. Some researchers believe it may have been Celtic in origin, although there is little documentation to support this[16]. Irish basketmaker and researcher Joe Hogan supports the Celtic-origins theory with linguistic evidence, examining Gaelic words still in use in Ireland to describe ribbed handleless potato baskets used today which are similar in shape to ribbed basketwork shields used there in ancient times[17]. The Celtic people seem to have originated in Eastern Europe and migrated west and east over Europe, beginning about thirty-two hundred years ago. If the Celts did develop ribbed basketry, their movement across Europe may explain why we find ribbed baskets spread over a wide geographic area: Hungary, Germany, Sweden, France, England, Ireland, and Scotland.

FIGURE 7
Ribbed willow basket, 23 x 30 x 18 cm, with a large diamond-shaped 4-point wrap and a wrapped handle made in the 1900s Normandy, France.
Musée des Arts et Traditions Populaires, Paris. 87.3; Neg. ATP 79.1.1382.

Because this style of basket was made by people for their own use, rather than by professional basketmakers, localized styles and traditions have developed with the passage of time.

Basketmakers in Northern France made a ribbed basket with a 4-point diamond wrap and overhand handle to gather potatoes and garden produce. (FIGURE 7) In Jean-François Millet's painting "L'Angélus," a couple stands in silent evening prayer, with such a basket, filled with potatoes, at their feet. Painted between 1855 and 1857, Millet's oil may be one of the earliest images showing the ribbed basket in use by French farm workers. A second Millet image, from 1863, shows a peasant woman on her way to work in the field, wearing the same style of basket upside-down over her head. (FIGURE 8) Such baskets were still being made and used in the

FIGURE 8

"Départ pour le travail," showing a woman with a ribbed basket over her head. Jean-François Millet. Etching, 1863.

Dartmouth Heritage Museum, NS. 73.87.81.

1980s on the French island of Belle-Ile-en-Mer—interestingly enough, by people with Acadian links to Nova Scotia[18]. French fruit-growers also used the hamper style of ribbed basket, with side hand-hold handles. (FIGURE 9)

There were other basket styles on the continent. Belgian Walloon basketmakers made a ribbed basket with a 4-point diamond wrap, which they called the "ear"[19] (FIGURE 10). Farmers in Spain, Portugal, and Switzerland also made ribbed baskets with variously shaped wraps, some with handles[20].

Likewise, there were several different styles of basket developed in the British Isles. Basketmakers in Scotland made deep ribbed baskets of twisted withies to carry peat, either on their backs or on donkeys. Irish potato farmers made a dish-shaped ribbed basket, called a scib or cis, for harvesting potatoes[21]. Another version, the *sciathóg*, was used to strain potatoes after they had been boiled[22]. This form is very common in Ireland; regional differences, such as the placement of the ribs in the framework, can be traced to specific valleys[23]. The Welsh had their own style of dish-shaped ribbed basket, called a *cyntell*[24]. Along the Cumbria and Dumfriesshire borderlands, this basket was called the "Cumberland swill." It was made of local willows by itinerant basketmakers, who travelled the countryside making swills for those who needed them[25]. Victorian

FIGURE 9

Hamper-style fruit-gathering basket, 33 x 127 x 54 cm, from the Sarthe Valley west of Paris, France.

Musée des Arts et Traditions Populaires, Paris. 91.3.9; Neg. ATP 79.1.1798.

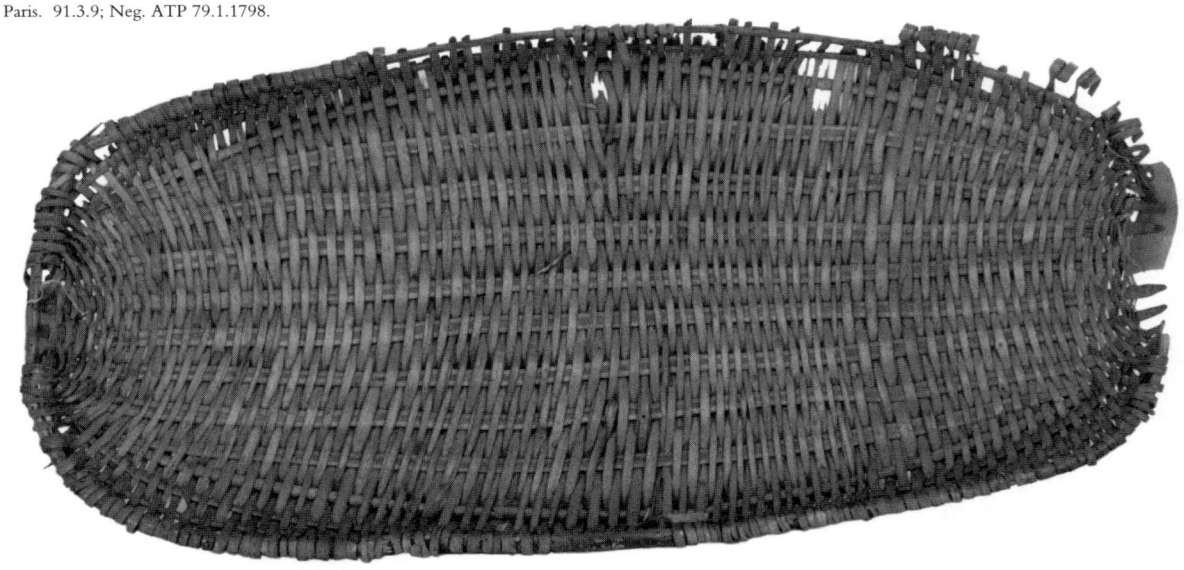

picture albums from Great Britain contain wonderful images of fishing and farming people using ribbed baskets in their everyday lives[26].

Some of these basket styles are still made in isolated pockets of Europe, while others are being revived due to current basketry interest. There are technical schools that teach basketry, and many basket festivals and interest groups keep the tradition alive.

Round and oval ribbed willow baskets continue to be used in green markets throughout Britain. Other shapes have disappeared, one of which is the spherical ribbed wool basket, or *mudag*, made by the Scots for wool gathering and processing[27]. Smaller versions made in Germany were used for gathering nuts, the enclosed shape being an excellent container for such materials[28].

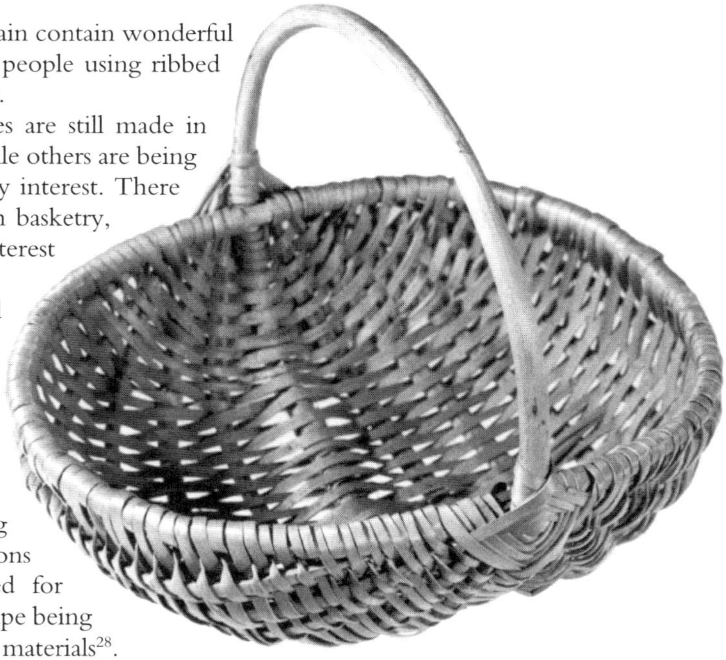

For the people of Great Britain and Europe who worked the land, the ribbed basket was the most common type of basket, and was made in various styles and sizes, with whatever materials were at hand. Willow was the most common material used to make ribbed baskets, but others were also used. In northern England, oak was cut to make ribbed "spales" or "spelks" for potato gathering[29]. Roots were also used to weave ribbed baskets. In Poland, frame baskets were woven with pine roots on a juniper wood frame[30]. Pine roots were also used in the frame baskets of the Cévennes in the northwest of France[31]. In Scandinavia, ribbed baskets of peeled and split root have been made both with and without handles[32].

FIGURE 10
Belgian Walloon basket, 18 x 19 x 17 cm, with the 4-point wrap known as "the ear."
Spa, Province of Liège, Belgium, c.1920
Rural History Centre, University of Reading, England. 60/7201.

The Ribbed Basket in the New World

IN THE 1500s AND 1600s, Europeans began to immigrate to the New World. They brought their traditions with them, including the craft of basketry. Missionaries of the Moravian Church, for example, brought ribbed basketry from Central Europe to the Danish West Indies, now the US Virgin Islands, as early as 1750[33]. The Moravians believed in teaching practical industries as well as providing religious guidance. When they came to the islands, they expanded the local Carib people's knowledge of making palm-leaf baskets with their own style of ribbed basket using native vines[34]. Production of these baskets formed a large, lucrative cooperative on St. Thomas, with markets in the United States and Europe. People continue to weave these baskets, with their dominant diamond wraps, in St. John and in Jamaica[35] (FIGURE 11).

Perhaps some of the earliest images of the ribbed basket on this side of the Atlantic Ocean are those by Camille Pissarro, in his market scenes of St. Thomas, Virgin Islands, between 1850 and 1855. (FIGURE 12) Better known as one of the leaders of the French Impressionist movement, Pissarro was born on St. Thomas; he was

FIGURE 11
St. John Market Basket, 30 x 48 x 29 cm, woven by Victor Sewer of St. John, US Virgin Islands. Note the handle and rim construction of peeled vine, the 4-point diamond-shaped wrap, the multiple sets of ribs, and the construction of the two lids.
Photo: Joleen Gordon. Private collection.
NSM N-25,357 #3.

encouraged to sketch local scenery before leaving to spend the rest of his life painting in France. These little-known sketches were lost to the world for many years, only surfacing in 1979 due to the diligent research of Richard R. Brettell, curator of the exhibition "Camille Pissarro in the Caribbean, 1850–1855"[36].

The tradition of making ribbed baskets also came to continental North America with settlers from Europe. In the Appalachian Mountains of the United States, for example, their descendants continue to weave baskets with white-oak splints[37].

In Atlantic Canada, there are four groups of people with a tradition of making ribbed baskets: the Blacks, the Mi'kmaq, the Acadians, and a small group of British descendants who lived on the Notre Dame coast of Newfoundland.

Black weavers living in Nova Scotia make both round and oval baskets of maple wood. These have a small X-shaped wrap, single and multiple sets of ribs, and turnbacks in the weaving. (FIGURE 13)

Most of the other Atlantic basketmaking groups use the larger, 4-point diamond wrap to hold the handle and rim hoops

FIGURE 12 [below left]
A detail of "Studies of People and Animals" by Camille Pissarro, 1850–1855. Drawn in St. Thomas showing a man carrying a basket. The outline indicates the shape of a ribbed basket with diamond wrap.
New York State, Office of Parks, Recreation and Historic Preservation, Olana State Historic Site, NY. OL.1982.302 (V).

FIGURE 13 [below right]
Market basket, 32 x 28 x 37 cm, woven by Esther Drummond of Cherry Brook, NS, in the late 1970s. The basket is made entirely of red maple saplings and the splints were dyed with birchbark.
Private collection. NSM N-24,622#8.

FIGURE 14
Oval-shaped melon basket, 22 x 25 x 38 cm, woven of ash-wood splints on an ash framework by a Mi'kmaq weaver of Maria, Québec. Note the large diamond wrap, the one set of ribs, the weavers turned around the rim only once, and the absence of turnbacks in the weaving. Private collection. NSM N-6798#11.

in their round and oval baskets. They differ in their use of woodland materials and a few construction details. The Mi'kmaq basketmakers on the Maria Reserve, Québec, use ash wood for the framework of their round and oval baskets, with one set of ribs and no turnbacks (FIGURE 14). The Acadian basketmakers of Caraquet and Madawaska in northern New Brunswick, plus those along the French Shore of Nova Scotia, make round baskets with a carved wooden framework, one set of ribs, and no turnbacks; the Acadians of Shallop Cove on the west coast of Newfoundland make their framework not of carved wood, but of peeled woodland sticks with one set of ribs and no turnbacks. Basketmakers who lived in eastern Newfoundland made an oval, carved-wood framework requiring multiple sets of ribs, which were woven with multiple sets of turnbacks.

The link between all these ribbed baskets is their European origin. The black basketmakers, descendants of black refugees who resettled in Canada during the War of 1812, trace their ancestry to the Chesapeake Bay area of the United States and to Africa. Basketmaking traditions stretch back in African history hundreds of years[38]. The ribbed basketmaking tradition is newer, possibly coinciding with European contact. In Virginia, Maryland, and Delaware, blacks worked tobacco plantations side by side with white indentured servants from Scotland, Ireland, and the West Country of England. The two groups lived, ate, and slept together[39]. This meeting of eighteenth century cultures may have facilitated the crossover of European basketry to the black community[40].

The Mi'kmaq basketmakers living in Maria on the Gaspé Peninsula are thought to have blended their basketry material of ash wood splints with the ribbed basket style of their Acadian neighbours in northern New Brunswick in response to the lucrative demands of the local potato-growing industry[41].

The Acadian basketmaking families on the west coast Newfoundland and those along the French Shore of Nova Scotia have both traced their ancestors to having emigrated in the 1600s from villages in Brittany, France.

The progenitors of basketmakers on the east coast of Newfoundland originally came in the early 1900s from the West Country of England—Cornwall, Devon, Dorset, and Somerset.

It is fascinating that, without exception, in all areas of Atlantic Canada where the Acadians wove these baskets, they were made in response to a need to gather potatoes. As we have seen from the documented pictorial evidence, this is the very same use for which they were made in France.

The choice of weaving material is intriguing. All the Acadian baskets and those made in British settlements on the Notre Dame coast of Newfoundland have been woven with split and peeled tree roots. It is known that this style of basket was woven with roots in Cévennes in northwestern France. Although it may never be known for sure, this style of basketry with this choice of material may have come to Atlantic Canada directly with the Acadians in the 1600s. On the other hand, it is possible that when the new settlers needed to make baskets to hold garden produce or their fish, Mi'kmaq or Maliseet neighbours introduced them to the long, flexible, and readily available tree roots. Recognizing the value of root as a weaving element, the Acadians combined a European basket style with a North American lacing material to make their distinctive basket.

Root Baskets of Nova Scotia

IN THE 1700s, Acadian life was tumultuous due to the warring French and English, who passed Acadie (now Nova Scotia, New Brunswick, and Prince Edward Island) back and forth like a ball. After the final fall of the French fortress of Louisbourg on Cape Breton Island in 1754, the English felt confident enough to expel the Acadian population. The Expulsion, or *le Grand Dérangement* as Acadians call it, began in 1755 and lasted until 1762. During that time, British soldiers burned entire villages with all their material goods to the ground. While most Acadians were deported to the American colonies, some fled to remote parts of Atlantic Canada—northern New Brunswick, Cape Breton Island, or Newfoundland—while others chose to return to France. Some later retraced their steps, settling in new areas, only to move again in a few years. There was an incredible amount of movement

FIGURE 15

Acadian baby basket, 30 x 41 x 67 cm, purchased from an antiques dealer in Pictou County, Nova Scotia.

History Collection, Nova Scotia Museum, Halifax. 72.351.3. NSM N-10,243.

within a very short time period, as the Acadian exiles sought new homes and a peaceful existence. They carried their cultural traditions with them.

The Nova Scotia Museum collection has two root-woven ribbed baskets, both of Acadian provenance. One is a large, oval-shaped basket without an overhand handle, which came to the museum with the name "Acadian baby basket" (FIGURE 15). The basket's history is somewhat clouded by the fact it has been labelled "Acadian," yet it was collected in Pictou County, an area of Scottish settlement.

So much has been lost but the basket tells some of its own story. Its shape is long and narrow, made carefully with sturdy materials. The carved-wood framework consists of two pieces of wood for the rim, their ends overlapping and nailed at both sides of the basket. Thick woodland shoots were peeled for the ribs, which run the length of the basket. The bottom is flat, so a baby could not be easily tipped out. Other shoots were peeled and used for the weavers, twisting the rods to make them bend more easily around the rim. These shoots have opposing leaf-scars down their lengths, so they are not willow, but they might be witherod (*Viburnum cassinoides*). The maker created two hand-hole handles, one on either side, so the basket could easily be picked up and carried.

The other root-woven ribbed basket in the Nova Scotia Museum collection is a gathering basket with an overhand handle, typical of the Acadian style. (FIGURE 16) It was collected from Digby County by Judge Philip Woolaver, who did a lot of circuit work in that part of the province. He thought this basket was unusual, so he gave it to the museum. Although we have no idea who made the basket, exactly where they lived, or its purpose, the basket has been very sturdily made and well-used. The two circular hoops of wood, carved from heavy pieces of hardwood, are intersected and nailed

FIGURE 16

Root-woven ribbed gathering basket, 23 x 24 x 26 cm, from Digby County, NS.

History Collection, Nova Scotia Museum, Halifax. 127.2. NSM N-24,620#10.

together, so the rim hoop lies inside the handle hoop, and are lashed together with the dominant 4-point diamond wrap. Eight large, carved wooden ribs are set into the wrap and woven with split and peeled roots, beginning with a thin root at the wrap and ending with wider roots in the centre. Over time and heavy use, the upper sections of the diamond wrap have broken away, leaving their ends projecting through the remaining wrap and revealing a lighter-coloured section of the once-covered handle. The rest of the basket is in good condition, attesting to the strength of the materials.

Between 1999 and 2002, Acadian basket research was conducted with members of La société historique acadienne de la Baie Sainte-Marie in the District of Clare, NS. Many inhabitants of this French Shore area can trace their ancestors to the original Grand Pré settlers who came from Brittany in France where, as we have seen, this style of ribbed basket was known.

The first language along the French Shore continues to be French, yet most people are perfectly bilingual. The names of the root baskets reflect trilingualism, however, showing a mix of English, French, and Mi'kmaq. They are known as *toubi* baskets or *panier de toubi*, with variants *toubie* and *tobi*[42]. The French priest Abbé Maillard recorded a similar Mi'kmaq term for root as early as 1750: "The finest fibril roots of the fir, which they called *Toobee*, and commonly use for a thread...."[43]. In everyday speech, the basket is described as having ears (*les oreilles*) and a mouth (*la bouche*). "Well, we had to give it a name," said George Saulnier. "It stuck out a little bit like an ear. Everybody that made baskets around this area, that's the name we had for it."

George Saulnier of Hectanooga, or George à Thanase as he is locally known, learned the craft of basketmaking from his family, where at least four generations of men practised the craft. He is the only person still making baskets, not only on the French Shore, but in all of Atlantic Canada.. George and his brother Simon learned from their father Thomas (Thanase), who learned from his father Leon ("Zoom"), who learned from his father Lange Saulnier. George's mother was born into another family of Saulniers in nearby Mayflower, Digby County, and they too made baskets. A third family of Saulniers, Moses and his four sons, also of Mayflower, made baskets as well.

Brothers Camille Maillet of Meteghan Station and Ulysses Maillet of Meteghan River also made baskets until the 1990s. They learned from their father, Albénie Maillet, and their father's brother

> There are relatively few **surnames** in Acadian communities so nicknames are used to differentiate. George Saulnier's grandfather, for example, was known as "Zoom." Acadians frequently add one or two generations of paternal ancestors after their names. For a recent novel about the people of Cape St. Mary's on the Clare shore and their use of names, see Betty Boudreau Vaughan's *I'll Buy You an Ox*.

FIGURE 18

Small root-woven ribbed basket, 16 x 18 x 19 cm, c.1870 found in Meteghan, NS, area. This basket is beautifully crafted.

Private collection. NSM N-25,212#2.

FIGURE 17

Vincent Maillet and his father Nicolas using a root-woven ribbed basket in a potato field in Mavillette, Digby County, NS, July 10, 1916.

Harold Robicheau Photograph Collection, Meteghan, NS.

Alphée, who in turn learned from their father, Théophile Maillet. The historical society members also remembered the names of two other root basketmakers: René Saulnier of Saulnierville Station who wove in the 1960s and Félix Melanson of Corberrie who wove in the 1930s. All their baskets were well used, and wore out with use, so that none remain.

Despite the loss of much local knowledge and history, some remnants were recovered. After searching through many photographic collections along the French Shore, one solitary image was found of a ribbed basket in use (FIGURE 17). As with many of these baskets, it was being used in a potato field. Society members also found some two dozen older root-woven ribbed baskets. Oral history showed these baskets had been made in this area for some four to five generations. The most common shape was the gathering basket. A small, very finely made basket with the honey-coloured patina of age was found in the Meteghan area (FIGURE 18). Two older, well-worn baskets are in Le Centre Acadien at Church Point, NS. Private collections continue to hold many baskets. Two large hampers made in the root-woven ribbed style were found, one in a barn being demolished in Little Brook (FIGURE 19), and another in a barn near Meteghan (FIGURE 20). They

FIGURE 20
Hamper-style ribbed basket, 29 x 45 x 58 cm, from Digby County, NS.

Private collection. NSM N-25,576#8.

FIGURE 19
Late 1800 hamper-style ribbed basket, 37 x 50 x 57 cm, found in a barn belonging to Louis Thimot, Little Brook, NS. Woven with split and peeled root on a hardwood framework.

Private collection. NSM N-25,212#5.

are very large, which suggests they were made to hold lightweight materials. Before he died, Félix Melanson remembered such large baskets being used to dry wool after it was washed, before being spun into yarn for weaving and knitting.

The members of the historical society in West Pubnico, La société historique acadienne de Pubnico-Ouest, found no root-woven ribbed baskets; but they did find two baskets made completely of root, except for the reinforcing hardwood rim and handles, in the Mi'kmaq wood-splint style (FIGURE 21). In the 1950s, Robert S. d'Entremont made two identical baskets for his sons, Paul and Sylvester. He used unpeeled split root with traditional Mi'kmaq construction techniques. He made a circular bottom by adding three sets of root standards, wove the sides with unpeeled split root, bent down the standards for the rim, and added two carved wooden handles on either side of the rim. The baskets are in good condition despite having been used for many years.

FIGURE 21

Mid 1900 root-woven hamper, 30 x 51 x 51 cm, made in the Mi'kmaq splint-basket style, by Robert S. d'Entremont of Lower West Pubnico, NS. Sylvester d'Entremont collection, Lower West Pubnico, NS.

Photo: Joleen Gordon. NSM N-25,103#15.

Another root-woven ribbed basket was found in Shelburne County. The Archelaus Smith Museum in Cape Sable has a beautiful little root basket believed to have come from the Yarmouth area. Because of pins and threads included therein, it was probably used as a sewing basket.

Hattie Perry, a historian from Shelburne County, once interviewed Charles Lamrock, who lived in Villagedale. Her notes describe how, in the early 1900s, he made baskets of black spruce root, which he collected in the spring and fall.

> These roots would be about 1/4 inch in diameter where they branched off the main root, and sometimes they would measure fourteen or fifteen feet long. He coiled them up and carried them home in burlap bags. There he stored them in tubs in the cellar, and kept them wet until he was ready to use them. When making a basket, Mr. Lamrock first fitted together the framework (handle and hoop) and the ribs. For these parts of the basket, he used split "Indian Arrows", which are tough straight saplings of the mountain ash, so called because they were used for arrow shafts by the Micmacs. He then selected the roots of the proper size (the larger roots were used for the larger baskets), and carefully pulled off the bark. Then with a very sharp knife, he split the peeled roots and wove them in and around the framework and ribs. The finished product was a sturdy round-bottomed basket.[44]

People remembered using these baskets for picking berries and for collecting eggs from the henhouse. Mr. Lamrock reported they were long-lasting baskets: "If they were kept dry, they were good for a lifetime."[45] There appears to be no one weaving root baskets along the Shelburne shore today.

There are many other Acadian communities in Nova Scotia, a few of which have produced root-woven ribbed baskets. Chezzetcook, on the eastern shore outside Dartmouth, is believed to be the origin of a root basket with some interesting variations. (FIGURE 22) This oval-shaped gathering basket has a simple X-wrap instead of the diamond wrap. It has not one set of ribs, but several sets, each inserted alongside the rim, creating bulging sides that require several turnbacks in the weaving. The maker chose the same width of root for the entire basket, making the weave pattern

FIGURE 23
Lithograph from an ambrotype of an Acadian woman from Chezzetcook, NS, 1859. Her Mi'kmaq style of wood-splint basket has a square-shaped handle set very low, somewhat like the handle in the root-woven basket below, also from Chezzetcook.
History Collection, Nova Scotia Museum, Halifax. N-8022.

FIGURE 22
Early 1900 root-woven ribbed basket, 21 x 30 x 28 cm, thought to have come from Chezzetcook, NS.
Private collection. NSM N-25,713#1A.

very fine. The wooden handle, possibly made of ash, is carved in a shape reminiscent of the Mi'kmaq splint baskets seen in two images made in 1859 of Acadian women from Chezzetcook, one of which is included here (FIGURE 23).

Recently, another much larger and more roughly made root-woven ribbed basket was found in the Acadian House Museum of Chezzetcook. The two hoops and one set of ribs were made of whole peeled sticks. The framework was lashed together with rope and woven with peeled and split roots. It is well worn and may have been used for clamming, an important local industry.

"A word in regard to the two **Acadian portraits**. They are literal ambrotypes, to which Sarony has added a few touches of his artistic crayon. It may interest the reader that they are the first, the only likenesses of the real Evangelines of Acadia. The women of Chezzetcook appear at daybreak in the city of Halifax, and as soon as the sun is up, vanish like the dew. They usually have a basket of fresh eggs, a brace or two of worsted socks, and a bottle of fir-balsam to sell. These comprise their simple commerce. When the market-bell rings, you find them not. To catch such fleeting phantoms, and to transfer them to the frontispiece of a book published here, is like painting the burnished wings of a humming bird. A friend, however, undertook the task. He rose before the sun, he bought the eggs, worsted socks, and fir balsam of the Acadians. By constant attentions he became acquainted with a pair of Acadian women, niece and aunt. Then he proposed the matter to them:

'I want you to go with me to the daguerreotype gallery.'
'What for?'
'To have your portraits taken.'
'What for?'
'To send to a friend in New York.'
'What for?'
'To be put into a book.'
'What for?'
'Never mind "what for" will you go?'
Aunt and niece—both together in a breath—'No.'

So, my friend, who was a wise man, wrote to the priest of the settlement of Chezzetcook to explain the 'what for' and the consequence was—our portraits! But these women had a terrible time at the head of the first flight of stairs. Not an inch would these shy creatures budge beyond. At last, the wife of the operator induced them to rise to the high flight that led to the Halifax skylight, and there they were painted by the sun, as we see them now"[46].

Cape Breton Island was a source of other root-woven ribbed baskets. Two large baskets were found in the village of Cheticamp in 1966, one woven of root and the other of wood splint (FIGURE 24). Characteristics of the baskets' overall round shape, size of the diamond-shaped wrap, one set of ribs, and shape of the ribs being wide in the middle and tapering to their points are similar to the Mi'kmaq ash-wood splint baskets from the Gaspé Peninsula. Cheticamp has always had strong ties with the Acadian communities of northern New Brunswick across the Gulf of St. Lawrence, so perhaps the baskets were brought from New Brunswick, rather than made in Cape Breton.

A small root-woven, ribbed basket in the shape of a football was collected in the Margaree Valley in the 1950s or 1960s by local historian Florence Mackley who displayed it in her textile museum for many years (FIGURE 25). She called it a wool basket or *mudag* and stated it had come from Scotland[47]. Although the basket is reminiscent of willow-woven wool baskets from Scotland, the use of root weaving material and the prominent diamond wraps

FIGURE 24 [below left]
Ribbed basket, 27.5 x 27 x 32 cm, woven with roots and a diamond wrap. Collected in Cheticamp, Cape Breton, NS, 1966.
Parks Canada 166.14.14. NSM N-25,764#5.

FIGURE 25 [below right]
Root-woven ribbed wool basket or *mudag,* 20 x 21 x 40 cm, with a diamond wrap. Replica of one found in the Margaree Valley, Cape Breton, NS. Made by Joleen Gordon in 1995.
Private collection. NSM N-24,621#9.

Three large wool baskets were found in three different collections on Cape Breton Island: Nova Scotia Gaelic College in St. Ann's; Beaton Institute of Cape Breton Studies, University College of Cape Breton, in Sydney; and Morrison's Restaurant, part of the North Highlands Community Museum in Dingwall.

on either end, plus the area it was found, suggest the Acadian style of weaving. Oral history from the basketmaking LeBlanc/White family in western Newfoundland shows that the family lived for some time in the Margaree Valley of Cape Breton after they fled Grand Pré during the 1755 Expulsion.

Another small wool basket with an unusual shape (not being spherical, but flat on one side, presumably so it could be carried close to the body) was discovered in Pictou, NS[48]. Several larger wool baskets, similar in shape to the *mudag*, and woven of whole withies and imported cane, were found in Cape Breton. This is not surprising, as the area was well-known for its woollen cloth production. Oral history records that the large wool baskets were used to hold teased fleece to keep it from blowing around the room. They were placed near the fire to warm the lanolin in the wool, making it easier to spin into yarn for knitting and weaving.

The Baskets of George Saulnier

GEORGE SAULNIER was born March 3, 1920, son of Mary Jane (Melvine) and Thomas "Thanase" Saulnier, in the family home in Hectanooga. George's grandfather, Leon "Zoom" Saulnier, was brought up in Meteghan River on the coast. He moved his family inland to Hectanooga in the 1800s, and they have lived there ever since. "I never went far enough," said George, "that I couldn't come home at night."

George can trace his ancestry back to the first Saulnier colonists who settled in the District of Clare, Digby County, soon after the Expulsion in 1755, when the British permitted Acadians to return to Nova Scotia. It is believed that all the Saulniers in Nova Scotia are descended from Louis Saulnier, a sailor who landed at Port Royal in 1683. Louis came from Ruca in the County of Matignon, Brittany, in northwestern France. The year after his arrival, he married Louise Pelletier dit Bastinaud, and they made their home at *la vieille habitation* in the Grand Pré area on the west side of the Canard River, which empties into the Minas Basin[49].

Genealogy of George Saulnier, basketmaker

Ralph Saulnier b. 25 January 1951

son of **George á Thanase Saulnier** b. 3 March 1920; m. Elfreide Margaret Comeau, d. 1 Sept. 1983; m. (2) Marie Estelle Deveau

son of **Thanase "Thomas" Saulnier** b. 30 May 1876; m. Mary Jane "Melvin" Saulnier

son of **Leon "Zoom" Saulnier** b. 12 April 1937

son of **Lange Saulnier** b. 19 April 1812

son of **Réné "le Jeune" Saulnier** b. 30 April 1769

son of **Réné "Poncy" Saulnier** b. 19 October 1723; m. Marie Madeleine Maillet

son of **Réné** b. 22 October 1688

son of **Louis Saulnier** b. 1663 in Ruca, in the old county of Matignon, in Brittany, France. He was a sailor and landed in Port Royal, Acadia, in 1683; m. Louise dit Bastinaud 1684. They settled at "La Vieille Habitation" in the Grand Pré area on the west side of the Canard River. (George Saulnier personal communication 21 September 2004)

The first Saulniers to settle in Baie Sainte-Marie on the French Shore of Nova Scotia were two brothers, Réné (b. 1723; m. Marie Madeline Maillet), and Claude (b.1724; m. Françoise Aucoin). (Nécrologie, LÉvangéline, 1891; National Archives Census Records, 1714)

George learned how to make baskets as a young boy by watching his father and grandfather.

> My father made baskets like this all the time. This was the only basket they had. There were no Indian baskets around, even in my young days. There was one Indian family, Elsie Basque's father, he made baskets for himself. He was a canoe maker, busy the whole year making canoes. When I was just a kid, seven or eight years old, I could see the others making baskets and I wanted to do the same. My father was shoeing oxen and I wanted to do the same. Made yokes and I wanted to do the same thing. When I grew up to be ten or twelve years old, I was doing things good.

Large baskets were used in the field to gather potatoes and in the orchards to gather apples. "Baskets, two feet across, we could hardly lift them when they were full of potatoes. Here, they had a lot of apple trees as well as planting potatoes and what they used for picking apples, they didn't use in the field because picking potatoes gets them dirty. Picking apples, they stay clean. So they had two kinds of baskets, them for apples and them for carrots and potatoes."

Smaller baskets were used to collect eggs. "My mother, she had hens and she'd sell the eggs. She would use a basket like this to go to the henhouse to get the eggs. And she would use one of these baskets to take the eggs to the store. They would use them for different things like that."

They made baskets primarily for themselves, but also for friends, and to barter as needed. According to Estelle Saulnier, "They also traded them for flour, feed for cattle, hay and vegetables. Like the Indians did with fur trading for anything that would help them survive and most importantly, to get to know their neighbours and get along with them...George's mother's side of the family also made them. Only three or four families, all related, made these baskets way back in the 1800s."[50]

George makes only one shape and style of basket, the round gathering basket with a single overhand handle. "I never made any different shape. I always made this kind. Well, I could make them square, I know I could. This is the kind I have always made." He has these baskets in a wide range of sizes, from very large to very, very small.

A detailed description of how George makes one of his root-woven ribbed baskets can be found at the end of this book.

Root Baskets of New Brunswick

ACCORDING TO HISTORIAN Bona Arsenault, Acadians returning from the 1755 exile settled in northern New Brunswick in 1785, clearing the land to grow potatoes[51]. Several large ribbed baskets with the diamond-shaped wrap have been found in this area, suggesting they may have played a role in the potato-growing economy. A smaller version used for needlework was found in the collection of the Musée Historique du Madawaska, in Edmundston.

People in the Caraquet area produced quite a few root-woven ribbed baskets. Two older examples are in storage at the Village Historique Acadien—makers and dates are unknown, but they are believed to have been made locally. Both have the circular rim hoop placed outside of the circular handle hoop, and both handles are unwrapped. One basket, with a wider shape and a low handle, has been heavily used and both upper areas of the diamond wrap are broken. The other basket has a higher handle and the wraps are in relatively good shape (FIGURE 26). A mark on the handle may have

FIGURE 26

Root-woven ribbed basket, 35 x 36 x 44 cm. Thought to have been made in Saint-Basile, Madawaska County, NB.

Village Historique Acadien, Caraquet, NB. VA 73.18.20. Photo: Joleen Gordon.

FIGURE 27
Handle marking.
Village Historique Acadien. Caraquet, NB.
VA 73.18.20. Photo: Joleen Gordon.

identified the owner (FIGURE 27), perhaps working in a commercial potato field. According to oral history in the community, although Mi'kmaq people made ribbed splint baskets in nearby Maria, only the Acadian people wove ribbed baskets with roots.

We believe that the Acadians relied on their friends the Indians to provide them with baskets. But as to every rule there is an exception and that exception was this man, Mr. Lazare Duguay from Lamèque who was making them. He told me that he had seen his grandfather and mother making them and he had some himself when he was a young lad. But it is only when he retired at 65 that he was looking for a hobby or something to do, that he recalled making those baskets and he started making them again. When I met him only a year before he died, he was making them almost full time and he was selling all of his production. The weaving material is split white spruce root, the elbows are made of willow and the handle and frame is made of split ash or sometimes he would bend the wood. Mr. Duguay died about two years ago [1980] and we don't know of any other Acadians that made baskets.[52]

The Baskets of Lazare Duguay

IN THE 1970s, Lazare Duguay made quite a few root-woven ribbed baskets for the Village Historique Acadien, to be used by site staff (FIGURE 28). He made large round baskets, with a heavy, carved wooden framework woven with split and peeled spruce roots. His widow reported that these baskets were quite common in the latter half of the 1800s.

> At this time, everyone in the region made some for their own use. They used them mainly in the field to pick vegetables, though some used them to go clamming. There were baskets for everything, either to pick wood shavings for the fire or to get eggs from the henhouse. The main way to make them is the same, two circles of ash for resistance, the ribs from little branching trees like the willow, all the rest are the roots of spruce trees, debarked and split. The connection of the two circles form *l'embouchure* [the mouth] and at the handle of the basket, you make *l'oreille* [the ear] in the shape of a lozenge.[53]

FIGURE 28
Interpreter at the Village Historique Acadien using a ribbed basket woven by the late Lazare Duguay of Lemèque, NB, 1982.
Photo: Joleen Gordon.

Hier l'Acadie, Scænes du Village Historique Acadien by Clarence Lebreton contains some wonderful photographs of Mr. Duguay's baskets being used by the guides at the village.

The terminology is interesting. Mme. Lanteigne used the words *l'embouchure* and *l'oreille* in the same manner as Mr. Saulnier on the French Shore of Nova Scotia. Linguistics is one of the tools used to connect people living in isolation. The fact that the same words have been used in both Acadian communities is a strong indication that these two communities may share the same source of basketmaking knowledge.

FIGURE 29
Detail of the back side of the diamond wrap, showing the nail joining the two circles of wood together.
Photo: Joleen Gordon.

FIGURE 30
Detail of the diamond wrap. Note the insertion of the root used to wrap the handle in the middle of the diamond which has broken away with use.
Photo: Joleen Gordon.

Mr. Duguay carved his circular rim and handle hoops of ash wood. He intersected the two hoops with the rim inside the handle, nailed them together, and bound them with a 4-point diamond wrap (FIGURE 29). One set of ribs, made of whole sticks of peeled willow, were braced between the inside surfaces of the two wraps. His roots were of the spruce tree, typically white spruce. He carefully chose a long root of even diameter, which he peeled and split to make the diamond-shaped ears (FIGURE 30). He added new root weavers by inserting the new end alongside a rib into the weaving (FIGURE 31). At the rim, he bent the weavers over the rim once, sometimes twisting the split root so the outer shiny surface faced outward, and sometimes not, so the flatter, inner side revealed the pith. When the weaving was complete, he slipped the end of the root under the weaving at the rim and finished by wrapping the handle with peeled and split root.

The painter, Claude T. Picard, living in nearby Saint-Basile, may have used one of Mr. Duguay's baskets with the wrapped handle as a model for his painting of the 1755 Expulsion used on the cover of this book.

FIGURE 31

New weavers were joined by slipping the ends alongside the ribs in the weaving.

Photo: Joleen Gordon.

Root Baskets of Newfoundland

TWO DISTINCTIVE STYLES of root-woven ribbed baskets have been made in two areas of Newfoundland for at least three, and perhaps four, generations: in the Acadian communities of Shallop Cove and St. George's near the Port au Port peninsula on the west coast, and in the British communities of Cobb's Arm, Virgin Arm, and Lewisporte on the Notre Dame coast.

Acadians from Cape Breton first settled in western Newfoundland at the end of the eighteenth century. By 1850, eighty percent of the people in the Port au Port peninsula and St. George's Bay area were French-speaking. During the 1900s, these people went through a drastic cultural and linguistic assimilation into the larger English-speaking community[55]. Through intermarriage, the skill of making root-woven ribbed baskets was shared by the Acadians and the Mi'kmaq. Anthony White (1915-1990) is credited with reviving the craft in the late 1970s. When he retired and needed a basket to collect his potatoes (FIGURE 32), he remembered the potato baskets made by his father and perhaps by others in the community (FIGURE 33).

FIGURE 33
Root-woven ribbed basket, 33.5 x 36 x 42 cm, with a diamond wrap, maker and date unknown. Collected in Stephenville, western Newfoundland. Some of the split-root weavers have not been peeled, making a darkened line of weaving.
Provincial Museum of Newfoundland and Labrador, St. John's, NL. 979.253.46.
Photo: Angel Deyoung.

FIGURE 32
Anthony White of Shallop Cove, NL, in 1979 with his potato basket.
Photo: Fran Innes.

The first people to come to Shallop Cove were the Aucoins from Margaree in Cape Breton. In 1849, Mr. Antoine LeBlanc arrived from Margaree. His brothers and sisters arrived in 1850, but they established in St. George's. His descendants still live on what was once his property. The early settlers were practically self-sufficient. They farmed all the vegetables that they needed. There was plenty of wild game to catch in the area: caribou and rabbit. Also there was plenty of fish. Herring was fished in the spring and cod in the summer. The herring fishery was important because this was how people purchased the supplies that they could not produce themselves: tea, molasses, beans, pork, salt beef and flour.[56]

Antoine LeBlanc's son Kenneth, also known as Canut LeBlanc, married Adelaide Benoit. Adelaide was a Mi'kmaq woman from Newfoundland who became well known for her basketmaking skills. Their son Antoine, known in later life as Anthony White, took up the skill, teaching his son Daniel. In 1996, it was with great pride that Daniel took his grandmother's skills to Conne River on the south coast to revive the craft in this Mi'kmaq community. Daniel continues his interest in his father's basketry.

LeBlanc family records show that during the Expulsion of 1755, the family fled to the Margaree area from Port Royal, where the original LeBlanc settler, Daniel, had landed in 1645. It is interesting that the records of two basketmaking families, the Newfoundland LeBlancs and the Nova Scotian Saulniers, share ancestral heritage in Brittany, France. Perhaps this explains why the baskets look similar.

Linguistic evidence shows that although he did not use the French basket terms used by Mr. Saulnier and Mr. Duguay, Mr. White referred to the 4-point diamond wraps by their English translation, "the ears." Perhaps earlier LeBlanc generations used the French terms of *les oreilles* and *la bouche*, which they anglicized, as they did their surnames during the time of assimilation.

Anthony White enjoyed making baskets for his family, typically the round gathering basket with overhand handle. The basket framework, handle, rim, and ribs are all made of whole sticks of peeled witherod or cherry. The two circular rim and handle hoops, made on a mould, are held together with a 4-point diamond wrap. There is only one set of ribs, with no turnbacks in the

Shallop Cove got its name from the French who often went there to load fresh water in their boats, called chaloupes. One night when they entered the brook, a storm came up and one of the boats was smashed up on the shore. In English, this term became shallop[54].

The **root basket class** taught by Daniel White included Howie John, Emily Benoit, Rocky John, Linda Stride, Tracey Stride and Carol MacDonald. The Conne River newspaper, *Miawpukek Aqnutemakn*, published "Basket Making—Reviving an Old Tradition" with photographs of the baskets and their makers. The article was reprinted in the *Micmac-Maliseet Nations News*.

FIGURE 34
Root–woven ribbed basket, 8 x 10 x 10 cm, made by Edward Young of Bay St. George, NL, c.1977. Note the rim hoop is *outside* the handle hoop.
Private collection. NSM N–25,724#10.

Genealogy of Anthony White, basketmaker

Anthony White b. 29 September 1915; m. Georgina Francis Tobin; d. 6 September 1990

son of **Kenneth White (Canut LeBlanc)** b. 1863; m. Adelaide Benoit

son of **Antoine LeBlanc** b.? Margaree; m. Marie LeBlanc 2 Feb. 1847 at Margaree; moved in 1850 to Shallop Cove, Newfoundland

son of **Marin LeBlanc** b. 1783 Margaree, Nova Scotia; m. Marie Cormier; d.1859 in Newfoundland

son of **Joseph LeBlanc** b. 1744 Cobequid, Acadie; m. Martine Arsenault

son of **Joseph LeBlanc** b. August 1712 Grand Pré, Acadie; m. Marie-Joseph Bourg

son of **Jean François LeBlanc** b.1682 Port Royal, Acadie; m. Jeanne Hébert

son of **René LeBlanc** b.1654 Port Royal, Acadie; m. Anne Bourgeois

son of **Daniel LeBlanc** b.1626 Martaize, France; immigrated 1645 to Acadie; m. Françoise Gaudet

son of **Alphonse LeBlanc** b.1590 D'Aulney, France; m. Jean Gaudet

son of **Pierre LeBlanc** b.1520 Martaize, France (Brittany)

(Rhonda White personal communication, 11 September 2001)

weaving. Anthony shared his skills with others, teaching Edward Young (FIGURE 34), and an evening class of young adults at Bay St. George Community College in Stephenville, NL, from October to November, 1980. One of these students was Eileen Murphy of Corner Brook, who has been a valuable informant for this study, and who continues to demonstrate the craft in Newfoundland.

Mr. White loved to travel with his basketmaking. He demonstrated at the summer fairs in Piccadilly on the Port au Port peninsula, and at a national craft exhibition in Toronto. In 1986, he was selected to demonstrate his craft as part of the traditional crafts of Newfoundland display at Expo '86 in Vancouver. Mr. White sold his baskets directly to customers and through the Beavercraft store in Stephenville. Colleen Lynch, who worked as a design specialist with the Newfoundland Department of Rural Development in the late 1970 to 1980s, wrote of Mr. White and Mr. Young in the Stephenville area making spruce root baskets in a style "which they relate was brought to the area by the early French settlers"[57]. Lynch also documented their work photographically.

Although they are not Acadian, the Notre Dame coast Newfoundland communities of British origin produced several root-woven ribbed baskets for a relatively short period of time, from the early 1900s to the mid-1960s. Laterally, Cobb's Arm seemed to be the centre of this activity, producing several baskets, including a beautiful root-woven ribbed basket in the 1930s, recently given to the Newfoundland museum by Mary Chalker. (FIGURE 35)

FIGURE 35

Clothes basket, 27 x 66 x 47 cm, also used as a baby cradle, from Virgin Arm, near Cobb's Arm, NL, 1930s, and possibly made by Phillip Pardy.

Provincial Museum of Newfoundland and Labrador, St. John's, NL. 2002.11.1. Photo: Angel Deyoung.

Cobb's Arm was actually the only place in the area where these baskets were made and they were known as Cobb's Arm baskets. They were made in several sizes, with and without handles. The one you saw was actually a clothes basket, not a cradle, but my mother found it a good way to cart an infant (me) around in boats. There were, of course, no roads at that time. It was given to me in the 1970s by my godmother who was clearing her parents' home in Herring Neck.

In our house in Cobb's Arm, there were two large baskets, twenty-four inches or more, with handles, by the side of the wood stove to hold two sizes of wood. My sister and I used to be sent with one to the landwash (the part of the beach between high and low tide) to pick up chips or small bits of wood used for starting the fire. We also had smaller ones (eighteen to twenty inches) but I can't remember what they were used for—usual basket things I guess.[58]

Woven of peeled and split roots, the Cobb's Arm clothesbasket, or baby cradle, shows details of basketmaking not found in the root-woven ribbed baskets made in the Acadian communities of Atlantic Canada. The handleless basket has a framework of two heavy carved pieces of wood—the oval-shaped rim hoop and the half-circle bottom hoop are intersected midline at right angles, with the rim on the inside, and are held together with a 4-point diamond wrap. There is more than one set of wide wooden ribs with thin tapering points. The initial set was placed in the wrap braced between the inside surfaces of the two wraps. Subsequent pairs of ribs were inserted alongside the rim as the weaving progressed outward, creating an oval basket with squared sides and a flat bottom. This shape required multiple sets of turnbacks to ensure the last few rows of weaving would be parallel along the midline of the basket. The addition of a twisted or "roped" handle to the rim is unlike handles on Acadian baskets.

Dr. John Sheldon, the area doctor in the 1950s, had heard stories of men making ribbed baskets of roots in earlier times, and he encouraged the current generation to revive the craft. According to his wife Kathy, the population of this area is homogenous, the people having come "straight out of Devon and Dorset" in England at the beginning of the twentieth century. The original basketmaking family was thought to be the Pardy family. Phillip Pardy, who wove in the 1930s, taught his son Doyle. It is assumed that Philip Pardy made Mary Chalker's baby basket, as Mr. Pardy and Mr. Chalker were good friends[59].

The Cobb's Arm basketmakers used wood from the aspen tree, *Populus tremuloides*. Hazel Hickmott, daughter of Phillip Pardy, remembers her mother "rinding out the rods with her teeth" to remove the bark; her father later used a vise for this chore, which must have pleased his wife. Alder rods, called "red rods, willies and withies," were also used. The handles were made by steaming and "bending them like ribs for a boat." Another feature is the diamond wrap, which was often dyed. Hazel remembers, "The dyes were not natural but were made with clothing dye bought at the store, mostly red."[60]. These baskets served many purposes: carrying wood and dried fish, berry-picking, cradling babies, holding coal, and storing knitting; they were not used specifically for potatoes.

Another hooded cradle (FIGURE 36) and several other root-woven ribbed baskets were found in this area, all having overhand handles, multiple sets of ribs, and multiple sets of turnbacks. One basket, known locally as "a traditional Newfoundland spruce root basket," was thought to have come from the Lewisporte area, not too far from Cobb's Arm. Two other baskets of unknown origin show such a strong resemblance to the Pardy basket and the Lewisporte basket that they must have come from this same area of Newfoundland, if not the same maker (FIGURE 37).

FIGURE 36

Root-woven ribbed baby cradle, 24 x 51 x 28 cm. Possibly made in eastern Newfoundland.

Provincial Museum of Newfoundland and Labrador, St. John's, NL. 986.93. Photo: Angel Deyoung.

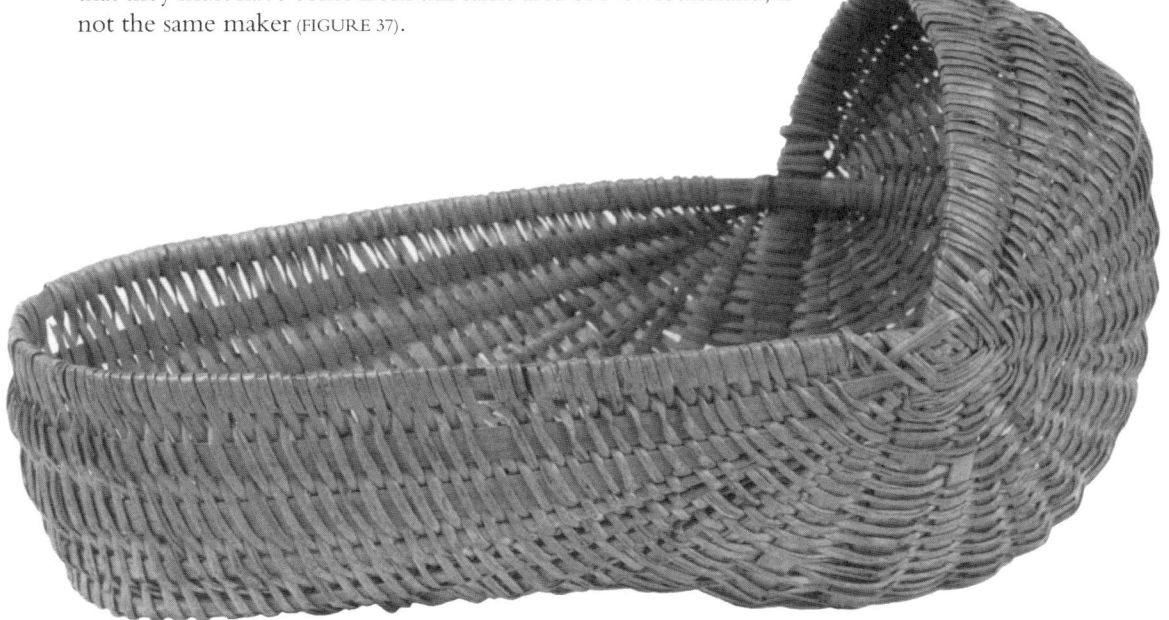

FIGURE 37

Root-woven ribbed basket, 25 x 28.5 x 25.5 cm. The basket shape, rib insertion, handle size, and notched overlap are reminiscent of other baskets from the Cobb's Arm area of Newfoundland.

Private collection.

Photo: Angel Deyoung.

Basketmaking was a cottage industry in the 1950s and 1960s for several Cobb's Arm families, such as the Woods, the Browns, the Blakes, and the Loders. The last known maker in Cobb's Arm was Frank Garfield Woods. He died on October 9, 1991, at the age of eighty. He had one sister living in Cobb's Arm, Gertie Brown. She shared memories of her family making baskets with Paula Gale, minister of the Herring Neck United Church.

> My parents and Frank made baskets in the kitchen of the family home. It would be full of roots and branches being dried and dyed and woven in the evenings. Frank made all kinds of baskets, party baskets with handles and two covers on each side, a trout basket with a hole in the cover, rough baskets, clothes baskets and smaller baskets with no covers.[61]

No example of Mr. Woods' baskets is known to have remained in Cobb's Arm. Two, however, are in the national collection of the Canadian Museum of Civilization in Gatineau, Québec, the smaller of which is included in their Canadian Souvenir exhibition (FIGURE 38). It is interesting to note that Mr. Woods used two different materials to make the hoops and ribs for these baskets. In the miniature berry basket, he used peeled whole sticks, while

FIGURE 38
Miniature root-woven ribbed berry basket, outside diameter 27.9 cm, woven by Frank Garfield Woods of Cobb's Arm, NL. 1960 ca.
Canadian Museum of Civilization, Gatineau. 894-2601.

in the full-sized berry basket, he made carved wooden hoops and ribs. In both baskets, the rim hoop is set inside the handle hoop, and held together with a diamond wrap made of peeled and split root. The small basket has one set of ribs, while the larger one has three sets. In both baskets, the peeled and split roots vary in size with finer ones near the wrap and wider ones in the middle. At the rim, the halved roots are twisted so that the outer, rounded surface faces outward, giving a smooth, shiny surface. Neither basket has turnbacks in the weaving. Only on the larger basket, much faded with time, can evidence be seen that the wraps were made with red-dyed roots.

The Baskets of Anthony White

The project "**Traces: Traditional Material Culture of the Newfoundland Micmac**," was initiated by the Provincial Museum of Newfoundland and Labrador in 1981, with assistance from the Micmac Crafts Committee and the Band Council of Conne River. It was in response to the paucity of material and documentation relating to the Newfoundland Mi'kmaq traditional way of life. Black-and-white photographs, colour transparencies, and audiotapes documented five crafts: shanks, caribou-skin canoes, snowshoes, spruce-root basketry, and costume. A final exhibit and a report of the same name were prepared by the museum in St. John's (Anger, 1983).

IN 1982, ANTHONY WHITE AND HIS SON, Daniel, were audiotaped and photographed as part of the Provincial Museum of Newfoundland and Labrador's "Traces Project." Root basketmaking was included in this study because Anthony's mother, Adelaide Benoit White, made baskets with his father Kenneth. The museum has a large, beautifully crafted root basket made by Anthony White, which has been displayed in their Mi'kmaq exhibit, "Elitagatiek," in St. John's, NL.

To make his basket framework, Mr. White used shoots of witherod (*Viburnum cassinoides*) or chokecherry (*Prunus virginicana*), which he wove with spruce roots. The photographs, unless otherwise credited, are the property of the Provincial Museum of Newfoundland and Labrador. The following quotations are taken from the "Traces" report[62].

> The first step is digging the roots and cutting the witherod. The roots of the white spruce are most commonly used. Red spruce may also be used but they are usually shorter (approx. four feet in length) than is desirable. Fir (*var*) roots are also used. They are lighter in colour and narrower than spruce roots. One digs with hands or a small garden trowel about three feet from the base of a fairly young spruce tree. Old trees are not suitable because their roots are too large and too tangled. After as long a length of root as possible is pulled from the ground, it is wrapped in a circle and fastened for storage.

Each tree has a broad network of roots, small and large. "The basket is very 'environment' friendly, in that harvesting of the roots does not in any way damage the parent tree. Only the fine roots (1/4 inch) are harvested, which leaves the larger more important roots to continue to feed and support the tree. Within a year these 1/4 inch roots return and can be harvested again."

In White's process, the roots are peeled immediately after collecting (FIGURE 39). Once dry, they would be impossible to scrape clean. If moist, they are peeled by hand, which is the easiest method. If they are drier, they are peeled or scraped with a knife. Wet peeled roots are stored in a sealed plastic bag for up to ten days. Dried roots are stored for a longer period of time, although their colour may darken. They are immersed in warm water to make them pliable for weaving.

After cleaning, the roots are split lengthwise. A smooth hand movement and practice is needed to split evenly without breaking (FIGURE 40). Thick roots are shaved to an even width and thickness along their length. Any width of root is usable, although for aesthetic reasons the roots used in any one basket are kept as uniform as possible. Narrow roots are used for the beginning of the weaving on both sides.

FIGURE 39
Anthony White removing bark from a spruce root.
This and the four photos which follow (Figures 40 to 43) were taken as part of the Traces Project in 1982, by the Provincial Museum of Newfoundland and Labrador, St. John's, NL.

FIGURE 40
Mr. White splitting a spruce root. Note that he has started at the thinner end of the root.

The witherod stalks are cut. Witherod or wild raisin is a bushy shrub which grows in marshy areas near the edges of woods. The stem is cut close to the ground and the leaves are trimmed off. The thickness of the stems chosen is kept as consistent as possible if all will be used in one basket. The bark is peeled, ends are cut blunt, bumps and irregularities are evened with a knife, and the cleaned stalk is ready for use.

As White's process continues, both the handle hoop and the rim hoop are formed around a mould. The facing edges of each hoop are thinned for about eight to ten centimetres (three to four inches) of overlap so the hoop is of even diameter all around.

The witherod must be three times the diameter of the circle—a 12-inch basket needs 36-inch witherod stems. The ends of the stem are tapered to a flat point so that they overlap smoothly. The witherod is nailed to a frame and the second hoop is wrapped on the outside of the first and nailed in place. The hoops on the mold [sic] are left to dry for a day. They can be baked in the oven for a couple of hours if quick drying is necessary, but natural drying ensures better quality.

Anthony White usually used a wooden mould, but in his evening class he used a plastic salt-pork bucket. In either scenario, both hoops are made on top of one another so that the first hoop is smaller than the second, outer hoop (FIGURE 41). Once dried, the hoops are removed from the mould. The overlaps are then glued and wrapped tightly with waxed string. To make the framework, the smaller hoop is inserted inside the larger one so that they bisect at their midpoints and at right angles.

Mr. White decided which hoop would be the handle by holding each hoop in turn and assessing the shape. This observation was given by Eileen Murphy, and it explains why some baskets have the rim hoop on the inside of the handle hoop, others on the outside (see FIGURE 34). This decided, the two hoops are tied together with waxed string and the first semicircular wooden template is tied into the framework.

The two hoops are then tied together using the waxed string at the points where they cross. The "ears" of the basket are then made. A narrow strip of spruce root is wrapped around the four points of the joint of the hoops. This makes a diamond shape which holds the hoops fast and provides a base for the insertion of the witherod ribs.

Additional templates are tied into the framework if deemed necessary, particularly on a larger basket (FIGURE 42). "Wooden semicircular templates are placed inside the hoops and tied in place from the top to bottom and sides. The templates—two or three, depending on the side of the frame—act only as guides for retention of the shape while weaving."

Mr. White then measured the lengths of flexible witherods for the ribs. The ends are tapered to a flat point and inserted into the ears. The ribs are placed about an inch and a half apart, depending on the size of the basket (FIGURE 43). They are positioned evenly across the bottom half of the framework and, just as George Saulnier does, Anthony White wraps each consecutive rib with a length of string to hold them in place during the weaving.

FIGURE 42
Tying two more semicircular wooden templates to the framework.

FIGURE 41
Mr. White preparing to bend the second witherod hoop around the first hoop already nailed on the mould. Bending the witherod between his thumbs along its full length gives the stick a memory, and makes it easier to bend around the mould.

FIGURE 43
Adding the ribs.

Beginning at one end by the ear, a narrow piece of spruce root is woven under and over each rib. The ribs are pushed down or pulled up with one hand while keeping tension on the root with the other. In that way, the basket retains a regular shape. When the first length of spruce root has been used, the other half of the same root is used to begin weaving on the other end of the basket. A second root, usually wider, is then woven into the first end. Its other half is used on the other end. By using one half of each root at either end, and working toward the middle, balance of size and quality is maintained throughout the basket. No knots are used in the weaving. Each row of root is pushed up by hand and ends woven double for a few inches. The tension holds them together. The weaving is completed in the middle and the last root is cut off close to the weaving surface. The templates which act as a guide for the weaving are removed as they begin to impede the work.

As Anthony White wove, each root was twisted at the rim to keep the outer root surface facing outward; he bent the root around the rim only once, not twice. The balance of the weaving was most important to Mr. White; he wove one half of each root on each side of the basket. When adding new roots, he sometimes overlapped new roots with the old for a few ribs and other times cut them so they met behind a rib. Because of the basket's round shape, no turnbacks were needed in the weaving. "These baskets can last for fifty years if kept dry and not given a hard time"[63].

Anthony White had been a carpenter all his life so he was familiar with visualizing objects and making things with his hands. With this skill, he looked at other styles of baskets and adapted them to suit his materials. There are stories of his laundry hampers, although none exist today; they have worn out with use. His daughter Jacqueline Snooks has examples of his experiments in weaving, such as wall pockets and a flower-pot basket. The most intricate shape was a fishing basket, known as a trout basket. He made the D-shaped bottom on a wooden frame, adding long ribs for the bottom and front, and shorter ribs for the sides. Then he added the lid with the hole for slipping in the fish, and lashed the lid to the basket with a split and peeled root.

Fran Innes published her article on Anthony White and his baskets, along with two photographs, in the local history magazine *Decks Awash*. Copies of this magazine are collected in the Centre for Newfoundland Studies, Memorial University, St. John's, NL.

Making an Acadian Root Basket Step-by-Step

THESE DIRECTIONS ARE FOR the traditional potato basket made by George Saulnier of Hectanooga, NS. (**FIGURE 44**) These instructions are for a basket 25 x 25 x 25 centimetres (10 x 10 x 10 inches). In the photos, you will notice George Saulnier is left-handed. The clockwise directions for making the basket's ears may be more comfortable for a right-handed person if done in a counter-clockwise direction; just make a mirror image.

FIGURE 44
George Saulnier, 1999.
Photo Michele Gallant.

STEP 1
....
Gathering and Preparing Root Materials

George uses spruce root gathered from the woods behind his home.

I don't know what gave them the idea of using roots. A hundred years ago, they used roots of the oak to hitch their teams of oxen to the carts. One piece of the yoke was made of roots. They made this big rein, all twisted together, one on top of the other, not braided, twisting it one on the other until they had a thing this big around and they'd put a pole in here to hitch the team on. And it was all made of root they dug out of the ground. So probably they said why can't we use roots for other things?

Roots are a wonderful material; they are readily available almost everywhere. Avoid collecting in rocky soils, where they grow crooked as they travel around obstacles; in open pasture land, or in woodland mossy areas, roots grow straighter. In good growing conditions, roots can grow at the same diameter for a long distance without tapering.

Use any root that will bend. The fir root won't bend when you come up around the rim; it will break. The hackmatack root will bend, only they are more reddish the root, they are not so white; the wood itself is quite red. My father used hackmatack root. The white spruce is the one I get roots from.

Hackmatack, also known as tamarack, juniper, and larch, is *Larix laricina*. White spruce is *Picea glauca*. Because of their toughness, roots are slow to rot, even in wet conditions. Trees have an elaborate system of large roots with an intricate network of smaller ones. Young roots are very fine, almost hairlike, while older roots are thick and woody. Basketmaking needs only smaller roots, and most trees can survive such a harvest.

The best time to dig for roots is when the sap is flowing, making it easier to remove the protective bark. George usually begins making baskets in early summer.

The last part of May to the last part of August. If on high ground, it will peel longer, you could probably go to September. On lower ground, the growth stops quicker. The growth of the tree, the sap, it stops flowing and you can't peel them. You gotta go amongst the young spruce—probably twenty-five to thirty years old. If you go after older spruce, fifty to a hundred years old, the bark will probably only peel for about two months, July and August.

In the early spring of 2002, when he was pressured to make several baskets, George experimented by boiling roots for about ten minutes to make them peel; it worked. Later in the fall, he was curious to try boiling the roots again, and again it worked. This experimentation has extended his basketmaking season.

George prefers to gather and weave his roots as he needs them. If necessary, you can either store the wet roots in a plastic bag in a freezer or dry them for future use to be soaked in warm water when needed to make them pliable.

To gather roots, select a medium-sized tree with a trunk diameter of 20 cm (8 ins) and begin digging a few inches below the surface a few feet away from the tree. Find a root of the desired thickness and pull on it from either end to see if it is straight. If it is crooked, leave it in the ground. If it is straight, cut the end nearest the tree and follow outward, pulling the root, ideally to the very end.

> **Boiling roots** to make them pliable is a technique that was known in the Mi'kmaq community. Andrew Paul told his grandson John Paul Denny of using boiled spruce root to stitch up an old time birchbark canoe (Whitehead, 2003).

I store them in water. Probably keep two to three weeks in the water with the bark on. Once you take the bark off, you use them. I never made any baskets with the bark on—it should look like hell if you was to make one.

The bark must be removed while the material is wet, preferably freshly gathered. Roots can be split either before or after peeling off the bark, a matter of personal preference. To split the root, insert a knife into the centre of the thinner end. Remove the knife, and with the fingers, separate the two sides of the root down its full length. It is easier to do this while holding the larger end steady between the knees, making the splitting action a combination of pulling up on the root and splitting the two sides evenly away from each other (FIGURE 45). If the root splits off centre, alternate hands holding the root and work as before. It may be necessary to insert the knife to get the split on course again. Keep the two halves together until ready to weave. George prefers to weave each half on either side of the basket; this makes the weaving visually balanced. Larger roots may be split in quarters to achieve the desired width. It may be necessary to thin the roots by splitting out some of the inner heartwood. Years ago, the thicker woody cores would have been saved for weaving heavier work baskets.

A big basket, to pick potatoes in the field, or apples. We used to have a lot of apple trees around here, all died because they were getting too old. We'd use the roots as wide as my finger, middle here, sometimes you wouldn't use the outside of the root. You'd split the root into three pieces and the middle pieces were cut on both sides, but you'd use that just the same, just a rough basket. So, you wouldn't have the smooth part on a bigger basket, you'd use the inside of the root, you'd use the split part on the side and the centre part in the centre, use it, strong, it didn't look so good as the rest, but it was fine for potatoes, get all dirty in the ground, laying down.

George used approximately 25 metres (80 feet) of root to make this basket. He collected all the root himself as it is not commercially available.

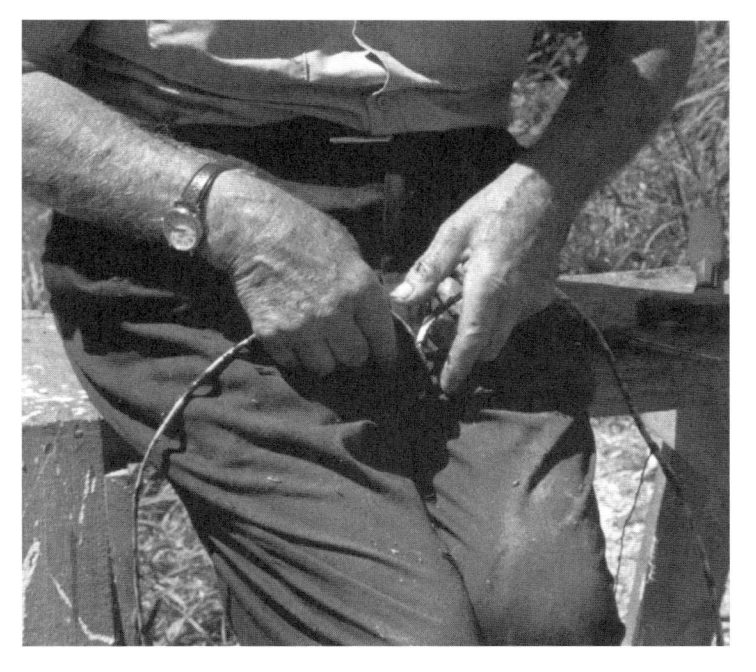

FIGURE 45

Splitting the unpeeled root by holding the root steady between the knees, and pulling upward and outward along the entire length of the root.

Photo: Joleen Gordon. NSM N-25,104#22.

STEP 2
....
Gathering and Preparing Wood Materials

For the framework of the basket, George uses either white ash (*Fraxinus americana*), or red maple (*Acer rubrum*).

> To get good wood, you got to cut it in the swale. Do you know what a swale is? Not on a hill, it's a hollow. It's a hollow on a hardwood ridge. It comes down in the hollow and it's soft ground. That's where I cut all my ash because it will never break. When you cut ash up on a hill, it's no good, it's brittle. White ash. I cut any size from four to twelve inches, whatever I can find. The bigger ones are best because when an ash tree starts growing, it's a little bit crooked and you cut it, you got that crook in your wood. As the ash tree grows bigger, it straightens out. Any time of year, winter, don't matter at all. A round block, I can keep almost a year before using it.

He cuts one-metre sections of the tree with a table saw.

> Take it to my workshop, I split it in two with an axe and then quarter it, probably two or four pieces to one half, makes it smaller, then I saw it with my bench saw, saw in strips, gotta be straight. If it's a crooked piece of wood, it will cut the grain and it will break. So you got to choose your ash when you go into the woods to cut it.

With a crooked knife, he removes the brittle heartwood and the outer bark before carving pieces for the handle and rim hoops (or "rings") and for the ribs.

> I cut them with the saw, pretty well the right size, a little thicker so I can smooth them off. Like this basket where the handle is quite big, you have to bend them on your knee. You don't want to bend it all at once, it will break. You have to bend it little by little.

George uses power tools to avoid wasting wood. In the days before table saws, Acadian men carved the wood by hand in much the same way as black Nova Scotian basketmakers carve red maple saplings for their baskets.

My father had to split everything by axe. And use his crooked knife. He always used ash because we have a lot of ash in the swale. First, they would split the tree in half, quarter it, split it into narrow pieces, probably two inches wide, and then take the heart out and that would leave the outside, about an inch to an inch and a half thick. Split out them pieces better once the heart was out of it. Take the bark off. Mostly used an Indian knife, the crooked knife. They probably used a draw knife on the big pieces. But on most of them, they used a crooked knife.

STEP 3

Constructing the Framework

Cut two pieces of hardwood, ash or maple. The handle is a little longer than the rim because the rim hoop has to fit inside the handle hoop. Cut the handle wood 86 cm (34 in) long and cut the rim 81 cm (32 in) long; both are 1.5 cm (3/4 in) wide and 0.7 cm (1/4 in) thick. Slowly bend each piece into a perfect circle and overlap the two ends by 5 cm (2 in). Shave down the inner or facing sides of each piece in the overlap to make an even thickness with the rest of the hoop.

Cut two sets of notches in the middle of the overlap. It is easier to mark the notches in both pieces of wood, release the wood and cut one set of notches deeper in one piece of wood, overlap the two ends again and cut the second set to match the first. Bind the overlap with string tied tightly through both notches (FIGURE 46).

Slip the smaller rim hoop inside the larger handle hoop (FIGURE 47). It is important to mark which is which with a pencil. Make sure the overlaps are placed where the two hoops intersect so they will be hidden by the ears. Move the rim hoop horizontally to the middle, making both sides of equal size. Then move the rim hoop vertically so it rests halfway on the handle hoop, giving the basket equal handle height and basket depth. Nail the two hoops together with one nail set into the wood on the inside of the intersection. Cut or saw off the projecting end of the nail. Repeat on the other side of the basket.

> I use a nail, but not in the small baskets; I just put a string. But quite a big basket, put a little nail because the basket works, sometimes it goes back and forth after you have three or four turns on the ear. I put a nail so if you go sideways, you can always bring it back, it stays straight, the nail holds these two pieces together.

FIGURE 46

Bind the framework hoop with string, drawing it tightly through both notches.

Photo: Joleen Gordon. NSM N-25,104#6.

FIGURE 47

Slip the smaller rim hoop *inside* the larger handle hoop.

Photo: Joleen Gordon. NSM N-25,104#11.

STEP 4
....
Creating the Ears / les Oreilles

Hold the framework so the intersection of the handle and rim hoops makes a plus sign (+). Select two halves of the same peeled and split root. Begin with the thinner end of one piece to bind the two hoops together, first in a simple X and then in a 4-point diamond wrap which George calls the "ear." Because he is left-handed, the root travels around the four pieces of wood in the rim-handle intersection in a clockwise direction. Think of them as the four points of a compass. Begin with the smooth, outer rounded surface of the root facing outward, slip the thin end between the two wood hoops on the bottom left (SW corner) and wrap the root diagonally up and across the intersection to the upper right (SW to NE) (FIGURE 48). Wrap the root around the rim (E), then wrap diagonally across the intersection and around the rim on the opposite side (W) making a simple X shape (FIGURE 49).

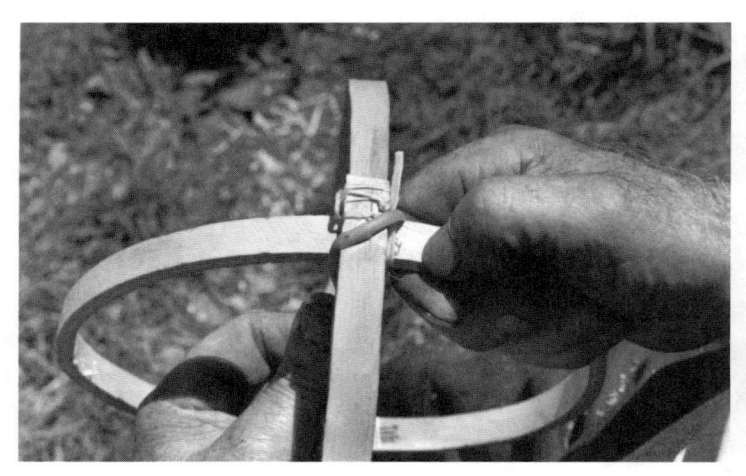

FIGURE 48
Slip the root under the intersection of the two hoops of wood and wrap diagonally to the NE.
Photo: Joleen Gordon. NSM N-25,106#1.

FIGURE 49
Second step of the cross wrap, completing the cross.
Photo: Joleen Gordon. NSM N-25,106#4.

FIGURE 50

The ear is complete.

Photo: Joleen Gordon. NSM N-25,106#6.

Begin the diamond wrap. Place the root to lie on the left side of the initial wrap and around behind the handle (N). In a clockwise direction, bring the root to the front of the work and wrap it completely around each of the four compass positions, E, S, W and N. Repeat this circle about seven times, each time laying the root outside the previous row so the ear grows outward. Slip the end of the root under the last row and pull it tight so it slips down between the rows; cut off (FIGURE 50). The inside view of the ear shows the nail set in earlier and the consecutive circles of wrapping beside one another.

Use the other half of the root to make an ear on the other side. In making the ears for this basket, George used a 4.7 metre (15 foot) length of root and he had a little over a metre (1.2 metres/4 feet) left over, so the ear took about 3.5 metres (11 feet) of root. The ears must be made large enough to hold the ribs. A smaller basket would have smaller ears.

STEP 5
....
Stabilizing the Framework

When both ears have been made, add a wire across the inside of the basket. Slip one end through the first four rows of the ear, twist the ends together on the inside, pull it tight across the basket and repeat on the other side (FIGURE 51). The purpose of this wire is to hold the round shape because as the weaving progresses, it often forces the basket into an unwanted oval shape. The wire is removed after the basket has dried.

> When you start making them, you are going to find it's a lot more problem than you think. You got to put a wire or strong string that won't stretch across the middle because when you pull on your roots tight, it kind of squeezes the basket together like this and it becomes oval like an egg. I made some like that years ago, before I started putting in the wire. They were coming out long and narrow. Then I saw my mistake, I saw what I was doing. You got to work with something before you understand it.

FIGURE 51
The wire across the inside of the basket.

Photo: Joleen Gordon. NSM N-25,106#15.

STEP 6

Preparing and Adding the Ribs

For a basket of this size, cut a set of ten ribs to add five to each side. Cut the ribs from ash or maple and shave each end to a long tapering point. Bend the rib so it is rounded (FIGURE 52). Brace the rib between the inner surfaces of both ears. Each pair of ribs must be cut to the same length. First, cut the bottom ribs to match the length of the bottom handle/rib (FIGURE 53). Then add the corner ribs, which are cut longer to make the corners well rounded; the basket will sit on these two ribs.

Finally, add three more pairs of ribs, each of varying lengths, to fill out the shape of the basket (FIGURE 54). To hold the ribs in place while weaving, tie a piece of string to the middle of the rim on one side and loop, do not knot, the string around the midline of each consecutive rib continuing to the rim on the other side (FIGURE 55). When this is completed, the ribbed framework is ready for weaving.

FIGURE 52

Bend to round the rib.

Photo: Joleen Gordon. NSM N-25,107#0.

FIGURE 53

Cut the bottom ribs the same length as the bottom of the handle.

Photo: Joleen Gordon. NSM N-25,106#20.

FIGURE 54

Complete set of ribs on the right side of the basket.

Photo: Joleen Gordon.   NSM N-25,107#5.

FIGURE 55

The string holds the ribs in place while weaving.

Photo: Joleen Gordon.   NSM N-25,107#7.

STEP 7
....
Weaving the Basket

Select two halves of a narrow peeled and split root to begin weaving between the closely spaced ribs. Slip the smaller end, with the outer rounded surface facing outwards, under a rib near the rim, then over a rib and around the rim. Twist the root at the back of the rim to keep the smooth, outer surface facing outward (FIGURE 56). Weave around each consecutive rib in an over-one/under-one pattern to the other side. Wrap the root around the rim, twisting it again, and weave the next row. The rows of weaving should alternate; ribs woven under in one row will be woven over in the next row. At first, the ribs may pop out of place; place them back in sequence and persevere. Weave equal amounts on alternate sides of the basket towards the middle.

> You start on both sides. If you was to start on one side and keep it going, it pushes the ribs; you'd have a big lump on one side as it pushes the whole basket. You gotta start from both sides, one here and one there. It keeps it going. Outside of that, it will throw it off course. The wood itself is green and you pull that root tight, it will push it to one side. You could start on one side and finish there but you would have a basket that is all one-sided.

FIGURE 56
Begin weaving with a small piece of root.
Photo: Joleen Gordon. NSM N-25,107#15.

Select roots of a size appropriate to the size of basket. Sometimes the halved roots might be thick and cause the surface of the weaving to be bumpy. If this is the case, take time to shave off some of the inner thickness.

You start with a small one, you try to keep them all the same thickness and not to have one higher than the other. That's why I shave the inside sometimes. When you split them off, they are a little too thick and you gotta take the inside, you got to take some of the inside out to bring it to the same level as the other ones. It takes a knack; you aren't going to make a nice-looking one first!

Eventually, all roots must end. George adds a new root by knotting the ends of the old and new roots together (FIGURE 57).

The fisherman's knot, that's the kind of knot to use—it never slips. I make a knot so I can pull it tight. You can shove the end in, but you can't pull tight on it; it pulls out. By making the knot, I can fasten the two together and keep pulling the root tight. Outside of that the root comes slack.

To make a firm knot, shave the inner sides of both the old and the new roots. Adjust their lengths so the knot will fall behind a rib. Pull the knot tight, cut off projecting ends, and weave in place. One important point: Knots are never made at the rim, as they can be seen, and may loosen with wear.

When weaving, pull each root horizontally between each rib so it fits as tightly as possible. The root is stretchy and therefore must be woven tightly so it will not slacken as it dries. If you feel the root getting dry and brittle, wet it with water.

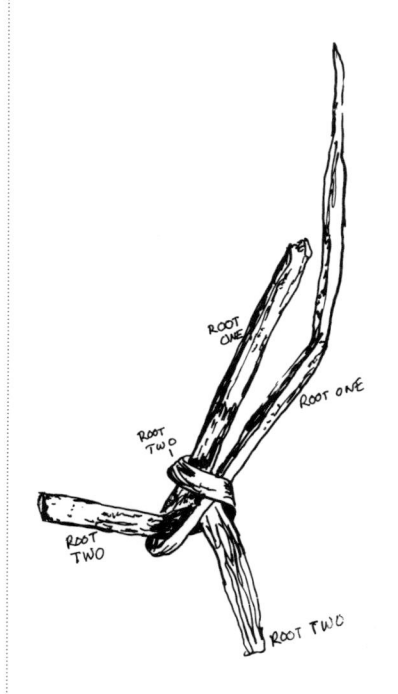

FIGURE 57
Diagram of fisherman's knot.
Drawing: Ruth Holmes Whitehead.

You gotta be fussy, watch all the time as you go along. When you put in your roots, you start pushing your ribs. You have to keep pushing your ribs back, keep shaping your basket until you are up a little ways on both sides of the basket; then it holds itself.

Take off the string when the weaving on both sides approaches the middle. The unwoven area may not be parallel due to the bulges in the basket corners. Pack the weavers along the centre bottom rib, almost turning them on their edges, while the remainder of the root rests flat on top of the ribs. (FIGURE 58)

> When it comes tight in the middle, and I can't shove my finger, I sometimes gotta to use a steel or a piece of wood that's tough enough to pull it through, but outside of that, I catch the roots with my finger; I put them right straight through with my fingers all the time.

One characteristic of these baskets is that there are no turnbacks. George uses a large screwdriver to force the rows of weaving apart along the bottom rib to make space to weave the remaining root. It's amazing; the roots slip sideways and the root weavers fall into place.

To end the weaving on one side, sharpen the end of the root and slip it horizontally into the weave under the rim (FIGURE 59). Cut off the end. Weave the remaining root from the other side so the rows of weaving alternate in the over-one/under-one pattern. End the other weaver in the same manner at the rim; it may be the same side of the basket but that is okay.

"The ends?" says George. "You can sort of hide the ends."

FIGURE 58 [left]
The two sides of weaving parallel in the central unwoven area.
Photo: Joleen Gordon. NSM N-25,108#5.

FIGURE 59 [right]
End one side of weaving at the rim.
Photo: Joleen Gordon. NSM N-25,108#7.

STEP 8

Wrapping the Handle

George covers the edges of the sawn wood handle, making it smoother to hold.

> Years ago when we made baskets, we never put the roots on the handles. The handles were bare wood. They smoothed the handles quite smooth, but they did not put on any root. That's a thing I started myself. I do cut the edges off the wood a little bit so it won't cut the root and so they won't bend square, they will bend round. I cut them a little all round, a little bit, so they will bend easier, so they won't crack. If you don't cut the edges off, the roots will probably crack.

Select a root with a width similar to the roots in the ears. Make sure it is long so there will be no joins; George used a root 4 metres (14 feet) long. Slip one end into a loop of one ear (FIGURE 60). Wrap the root tightly around the handle, making the rows close together, to the other side. Shave off some inner thickness and slip the end into the weave of the other ear. Pull it down tight into the ear pattern and cut off (FIGURE 61).

> I had to add, I had to take two roots to wrap this handle. Where you stop, you have to leave a piece so when you start with the second one, before you start with your second root, the first root has to wind two or three turns on the second root to catch it, so it will stay and it don't show. It might show a little bit, but it's quite smooth. Here I have it small on both sides and big in the middle. Why sure, it makes it look good. I started with the small end and when I got here, it got big and the second root I started here with the big end here and finished with the small end there. You have to think a lot.

FIGURE 60
Begin to wrap the handle with root.
Photo: Joleen Gordon.
NSM N-25,108#13.

FIGURE 61
End of handle wrap.
Photo: Joleen Gordon.
NSM N-25,108#15.

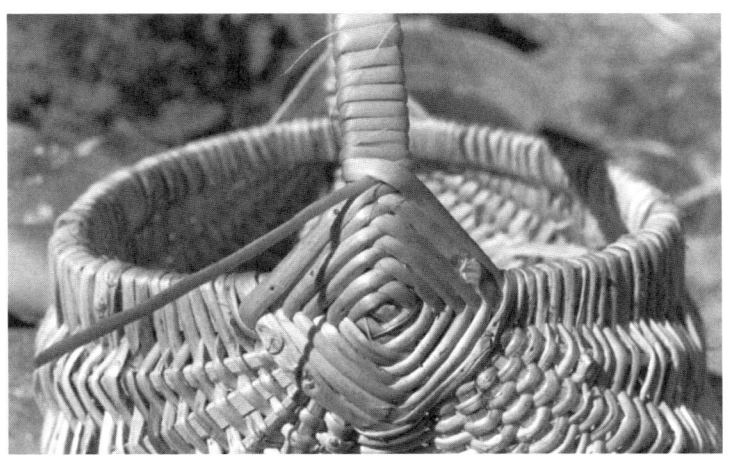

STEP 9

Drying and Using

Dry the basket in a place with good air circulation to prevent moulding. When the basket has dried, in a day or so, remove the inner wire (FIGURE 62). The wood is left as is—George never coats the basket with stain or varnish.

These baskets are built to last. They are the result of many years of experimentation by many basketmakers playing with their materials, forms, and functions.

> If the roots get dry, real dry, then they break easy. If you was to lay it down on the ground roughly, it could hit a stone, it could cut it. But they last? Oh geez, I don't know—forever. They never rot. If you are easy with them, take care of them, they will do the lifetime of a person. I like making them.

FIGURE 62
George Saulnier with his completed basket, 27 x 23 x 25 cm, August 4, 1999.
Photo: Joleen Gordon. NSM N-25,108#18.

Conclusion

THIS IS THE FIRST ATTEMPT to identify the root-woven ribbed basket with the large diamond wrap as part of the Acadian material culture in Atlantic Canada. During the five years of searching Atlantic Canada and the national Canadian collection in Gatineau, Québec, a total of seventy-five root baskets were examined and the names of several basketmakers recorded in Nova Scotia, New Brunswick, and Newfoundland. Of the basket total, the majority (sixty-nine) were linked to people of Acadian descent; the remaining six were made by a small group of people with British heritage in Notre Dame, Newfoundland.

The three Acadian men profiled–George Saulnier of Hectanooga, Nova Scotia; Lazare Duguay of Lamèque, New Brunswick; and Anthony White of Shallop Cove, Newfoundland–all learned basketmaking from their fathers and grandfathers. Records of the Saulnier and White/LeBlanc families showed they emigrated from Brittany in France in the late 1800s, settling in the Grand Pré area of Nova Scotia. As this basket style was known in France, some woven with roots and others with withes, it is possible the Acadians made these root baskets at the time of settlement in the New World. During the Expulsion, they carried this skill with them and started making these baskets when they resettled in other communities of Atlantic Canada.

The common basket shape in the Acadian communities was a round gathering basket with an overhand handle. The method of construction was the same, two hoops intersecting at right angles and held together with a 4-point diamond wrap on either side of the basket, between which one set of ribs was braced. The weaving material was tree root, peeled and split in half. The method of weaving was the same, beginning at each wrap on either side of the basket, continuing on each consecutive rib in an over-one/under-one pattern, and ending along the midline of the basket. Each time the root turned around the rim, it was given a twist so that the convex outer surface remained facing outward. In addition, two hamper-style baskets without an overhand handle were found, plus a spherical wool basket.

In making the gathering basket, there were some differences, possibly due to the materials, the cultural background of the basketmaker, or the personal preference of the maker. For instance, the basket framework was made of carved hardwood in all areas except western Newfoundland, where basketmakers used whole sticks of woodland shrubbery. This may have been due to availability of materials, as western Newfoundland does not have many hardwood trees. Another major difference was the shape of the basket which, in turn, dictated the number of sets of ribs. In all Acadian locations, the basket framework was melon-shaped, requiring one set of ribs. In Notre Dame, Newfoundland, the basket was square shaped, which required multiple sets of ribs. This may have been due to the cultural difference between the Acadian and British origins of these respective communities.

A more subtle difference was found in the final treatment of the handle. All of the older baskets from all areas had unwrapped handles. Two recent Acadian basketmakers, Lazare Duguay in northern New Brunswick, and George Saulnier of the French Shore in Nova Scotia, wrapped their handles with split root. This was likely a matter of personal preference. Unfortunately, Mr. Duguay had passed away before this study was undertaken, so it is unclear as to why he wrapped his handles, but Mr. Saulnier related that he wrapped his handles to cover the harsh edges of the sawn-wood framework, thus making the basket easier to hold and to use.

The Acadians who made these baskets worked for many generations making baskets for themselves and for their neighbours. Because the basket is similar to other ribbed baskets made by Mi'kmaq and black basketmakers in Atlantic Canada, as well as to the ribbed baskets made in the Appalachian Mountains of the United States, some people may feel the Acadians learned basketmaking from another cultural group. There are several arguments against this line of thought.

The Acadians and the Mi'kmaq have always lived close to one another, the early settlers acquiring many of their survival skills. Although root was one of the basketry materials used in Cévennes, France, the Acadians may have adopted the Mi'kmaq use of root to weave their baskets. It is highly unlikely that the Mi'kmaq taught ribbed basketry to the Acadians. Most Mi'kmaq are unfamiliar with this ribbed style of basket, and those that did weave the ribbed basket in northern New Brunswick reported learning it recently—in the 1930s—probably as an economic response to the nearby potato industry. Oral histories of Acadians from three provinces, and a Nova Scotian photograph from 1910 show that the Acadians were making root-woven ribbed baskets well before the 1930s.

The Acadians did not learn basketry from black basketmakers, either. There are too many differences in their basket styles: the shape of the wrap, the shape of the basket, the multiple sets of ribs, the use of turnbacks, and the materials. The two cultural groups rarely crossed paths, and even then a few members might have met only at the Halifax Farmers' Market. Only the Acadians who lived in Chezzetcook regularly attended this market. It is interesting that the one basket attributed to Chezzetcook, although woven with root, has an oblong shape with multiple sets of ribs like the black baskets and a carved wooden handle much like the Mi'kmaq baskets.

It is also unlikely that the Acadians learned from basketmakers in the Appalachian Mountains. While Acadians may have returned from Louisiana through the mountains, some families, like the LeBlancs, never went to the United States; they fled Grand Pré to Cape Breton and then to Newfoundland. Others, like the Saulnier family, were exiled from Grand Pré to Massachusetts, far north of the main Appalachian basketmaking areas, before returning to the French Shore of Nova Scotia. Yet both families have been making root-woven ribbed baskets for three or four generations, if not more.

Linguistic evidence reveals the ribbed basket's links, not only between the Acadian communities of eastern Canada, but also between Atlantic Canada and Europe. Acadian basketmakers along the French Shore of Nova Scotia, in Caraquet, New Brunswick, and in Shallop Cove, Newfoundland, all called the 4-point diamond wraps *les oreilles*, or "the ears." This terminology is still used in Europe today, as evidenced by the Belgian Walloon basketmakers who call the same diamond pattern the "ear." Basketmakers on the east coast of Newfoundland used neither the French terms nor their translations. Their words demonstrated their British heritage: the 4-point wrap was a diamond, and the flexible materials were withies, willies or red rods. They also spoke of "rinding out" the material, meaning to peel off the bark, again a British phrase.

All evidence indicates the Acadians brought their craft of basketmaking directly from France. It is interesting that two of the basketmaking families interviewed, one in Nova Scotia and the other in western Newfoundland, can trace their ancestors back to Brittany in northwestern France. Both families then settled around Port Royal, Nova Scotia, in the mid- to late 1600s.

This story of the root-woven ribbed basket has expanded the basketry knowledge of Atlantic Canada. Evidence from oral history, surviving artifacts, and linguistics has proven that the Acadians had a well-established basket tradition in several communities of eastern Canada. Research also revealed basketry activity with British origins, which has since disappeared, on the Notre Dame coast of Newfoundland.

The Acadian style of basket is in danger of dying out of the oral tradition. As recently as ten to twenty years ago, there were several basketmakers weaving on the French Shore of Nova Scotia, in northern New Brunswick, and in western Newfoundland. Today, only one Acadian man continues this tradition, George Saulnier of Hectanooga, Nova Scotia. It is hoped that this study will encourage people to learn how to gather roots and weave, thus keeping the skill of making these beautiful baskets alive in Atlantic Canada.

Appendix

The following individuals and organizations may offer root basketry classes:

Nova Scotia

Société historique acadienne de la Baie Sainte-Marie
  Université Sainte Anne, Church Point B0W 1M0

Nova Scotia Basketry Guild
Joleen Gordon, 121 Crichton Ave.,
  Dartmouth B3A 3R6

New Brunswick

Village Historique Acadien Box 5626 Caraquet E1W 1B7
  Sylvan Gaudet 506-726-2600

Newfoundland

Danny White, P.O. Box 24, Havelock, Ontario K0L 1Z0
  705-778-1741

Eileen Murphy, 1 Armstrong Ave., Corner Brook
  709-634-3304

Notes

INTRODUCTION

1. Whitehead, 1986; Gordon, 1993; Gordon, 1995; Gordon, 1997
2. Whitehead, 1980: 54-67; Gordon, 1990: 17-44
3. Dupont, 1978: 283, 291
4. Gordon, 1984
5. Gordon, 1981
6. Gordon, 1977

ROOT: MOTHER NATURE'S THREAD

7. Ågren and Lundholm, 1976; Stewart, 1984: 171-177; Paul, 1991; Hasselrot, 1997
8. McGhee, 1996: 218, plate 16
9. Wallace, 1991: 183-185
10. Whitehead, 1987: 38-40; Marshall, 1996: 321-326
11. Lescarbot, 1928: 423
12. qtd. in Wallis and Wallis, 1955: 73-74

THE RIBBED BASKET

13. All Saulnier quotes come from interviews 11 July 1999, 3 August 1999, 24 October 1999, 27 August 2002, and 21 September 2004.
14. Wright, 1983: 25
15. Duchesne, Ferrand and Thomas, 1981: 156-162
16. Wright, 1983: 23-25; Law and Taylor, 1991: 65-122; Gabriel and Goyner, 1991: 29-31; Butcher, 1999: 79
17. Hogan, 2001: 289-295
18. Griffiths, 1981a; 1981b
19. Delvaux, 1934-35; Wright, 1983: 122
20. Verdet-Fierz, 1993: 244-255
21. Shaw-Smith, 1984: 118-129
22. Fitzgerald, 1986 and 1987; Hogan, 2001: 86-91
23. Butcher, 1999: 79
24. Davies, 1999
25. Fuller, 1998
26. Fitzgibbon, 1970; Thompson, 1976; Creasey, 1977
27. Grant, 1961: 209; Morris and Cheape, 2000: 86-91

28 Thierschmann, 1996
29 Barratt, 1983
30 Butcher, 1991: 31
31 Butcher, 1999: 79
32 Hasselrot, 1997: 148-157; 1998
33 Kemp, 1990
34 Oldendorp, 1987: 18
35 Guth, 1982
36 Brettell, Zukowski and Pissaro, 1996
37 Eaton, 1973: 166-178; Stephenson, 1977: 12-30; Irwin, 1982: 43-60; Law and Taylor, 1991: 65-122
38 Etienne-Nugue, 1982; 1985; 1987; 1990
39 Ferguson, 1992: 41-44
40 Gordon, 1977
41 Pelletier, 1973; Gaby Pelletier, personal communication, 3 December 2002

ROOT BASKETS OF NOVA SCOTIA

42 Thibodeau, 1988: 124; Cormier, 1999: 365-366
43 Whitehead, 1982: 73
44 Perry, 1989: 28
45 Perry, 1989:28
46 Cozzens 1877: iv-v
47 Mackley, 1977: 18
48 Gordon, 1984: 13
49 George Saulnier personal communication, 10 July 1999
50 Estelle Saulnier personal communication, January 1999

ROOT BASKETS OF NEW BRUNSWICK

51 Arsenault, 1978: 233-236
52 Thérèse Thériault personal communication, 20 December 1982
53 Délanda Lanteigne personal communication, 24 November 1982. Translated by Violet Gaudet)

ROOT BASKETS OF NEWFOUNDLAND

54 "Carpe Diem: Tempus Fugit," 1978, 1:8
55 Matthews, 1976: 84-119
56 "Carpe Diem: Tempus Fugit," 1978, 2:148-149
57 Lynch, 1979: 16
58 Mary Chalker personal communication, 27 July 2002
59 Kathy Sheldon personal communication, 15 October 2002
60 Hazel Hickmott qtd. by Kathy Sheldon, personal communication, 15 October 2002
61 Gertie Woods qtd. by Paula Gale, personal communication, 5 October 2002
62 Anger, 1983
63 Innes, 1979: 61

Acknowledgements

THIS PROJECT WAS FUNDED with research grants from the Nova Scotia Museum and the Helen Creighton Folklore Society, for which I am very grateful. I owe special thanks to Michele Gallant who assisted me with photographing Mr. Saulnier and to my daughter Heather Gordon McLean who assisted with French translations. I thank my colleagues at the Nova Scotia Museum for their support: Scott Robson, Ruth Holmes Whitehead, Etta Moffatt, David Christianson, Alex Wilson and Marian Munro; I also thank Roger Lloyd and Richard Plander, Nova Scotia Department of Education's Learning Resources and Technology, for their diligent photographic work. Grateful thank you to Sandra McIntyre and the staff of Nimbus and to Kathy Kaulbach who made this book a reality.

This book would not have been possible without people telling me their stories; I owe them each a debt of gratitude.

NOVA SCOTIA

The people along the French Shore found several baskets in their homes and barns. They were patient with all my questions. I made many friends. I thank George and Estelle Saulnier of Hectanooga for their faith in me. Basket stories came from Ron and Darlene Gillis, Meteghan; members of Société historique acadienne de la Baie Sainte-Marie; Jean Doucet, Concession; Emile Dugas, Concession; Loretta Blinn, Ohio; Herbert Boudreau, Grosses Coques; Antoinette Benoit Comeau, Little Brook; Ulysses Maillet, Meteghan River; Camille Maillet, Meteghan Station; Violet Gaudet, Little Brook; Marie-Adèle Deveau, Meteghan River; Lydia Saulnier, Saulnierville; Judge Philip Woolaver, Bear River; Howard Benham, Yarmouth; Elaine Surette and members of La Société Historique Acadienne de Pubnico-ouest; Paul and Sylvester d'Entremont, Lower West Pubnico; Heather Atkinson and Margaret Messenger, Archelaus Smith Museum, Clark's Harbour. The only photograph found that shows the use of the basket along the shore was from the collection of Harold Robicheau, Meteghan. For my work in the Chezzetcook area, I thank Lene Fergusson of West Chezzetcook for help with local history and Ruth Edsall of Halifax for sharing her basket and its story from this community.

Colleagues in other museums were patient as I searched their collections: Gérald Boudreau, Centre Acadien in Church Point;

Eric Ruff, Yarmouth County Museum; Pauline d'Entremont and Bernice d'Entremont, Musée Acadien de Pubnico-Ouest; Sandy Balcom, Fortress Louisbourg; Anita Campbell, Brenda Dunn and Birgitta Linderoth Wallace Ferguson, Parks Canada in Halifax; Charlene Kosick, Highland Village Museum; Heather Morrison, North Highlands Community Museum; Dora Carrigan, Margaree Bicentennial Museum; Anita Price and Faith Wallace, Dartmouth Heritage Museum; and Sandra Winter, Kempt Shore, NS.

NEW BRUNSWICK

Basket stories came from Madame Lazare Duguay, in a letter from Délanda Lanteigne of Bathurst to the late Marian DeWitt; Thérèse Thériault and Sylvan Gaudet of the Village Historique Acadien in Caraquet; Gilbert Lavoie, Musée Historique du Madawaska in Edmunston, Gaby Pelletier, formerly of the New Brunswick Museum, and Colleen Lynch, Chamcook. Assistance with Acadian genealogy and history was given by Steven White and Ronald LaBelle, Centre d'Etudes Acadiens, while Bernard LeBlanc of the Acadian Museum at the University of Moncton guided me through that collection. The artist Claude T. Picard, Saint Basile, graciously gave me permission to use one of his images to illustrate this story.

PRINCE EDWARD ISLAND

George Arsenault of Miscouche and Cecile Gallant of the Acadian Museum assisted with my search.

NEWFOUNDLAND

I owe a debt of gratitude to the family of Anthony White: Jacqueline Snooks, Flat Bay; Kenneth and Shirley White and Clayton and Gail White, Shallop Cove; Daniel White, Norwood, Ontario; and Rhonda White, St. George's. Newfoundland's west-coast basketry stories were broadened by information from Fran Innes, St. John's; Helga Gillard, Main Brook; Eileen Murphy, Cornerbrook; and Paula Cornec, Stephenville. Notre Dame coast basketry stories came from Mary and Georgie Chalker, St. John's; John and Kathy Sheldon, Virgin Arm; Gertie Woods Brown, Cobb's Arm; and the Rev. Paula Gale, Cobb's Arm.

For their patience with my basket-sleuthing in their collections, I thank my colleagues Elaine Anton, Blair Withycombe, Mark Ferguson and Angel Deyoung, Provincial Museum of Newfoundland and Labrador; Diane Tye, Memorial University; and Sharon LeRiche, Craft Council of Newfoundland and Labrador.

OUTSIDE ATLANTIC CANADA

Trips to Gatineau, Montréal and Québec City broadened my search. I thank Stephen Augustine, Robert McGhee, Pat Sutherland and Peter Rider, Canadian Museum of Civilization; Moira McCaffrey, McCord Museum; Sister Nicole Perron, Musée des Augustines in Québec City; and Betty Martin of the Maria Cooperative. I also thank Naomi Griffiths of Ottawa.

Research colleagues in the United States included Warren Perrin, CODOFIL in Louisiana; Ronna Dixon, New York State Office of Parks, Recreation and Historic Preservation in Waterford; Bernard Kemp and Ralph Prince in the US Virgin Islands.

This study extended beyond North America. In France, Martine Jaoul, Direction Régionale des Affaires Culturelles, Toulouse; Jocelyn Etienne-Nugue, UNESCO in Paris; Brigitte Lozza, Musée National des Arts et Traditions Populaires in Marseille; and Helene Balfet, Musée de l'Homme in Paris. In Great Britain, Mary Butcher, Canterbury in England; Alison Fitzgerald, Loughgall, and Joe Hogan, Clonbur in Ireland; Alex Bury, Craven Arms in England; and Hugh Cheape, National Museum of Scotland in Edinburgh. Earlier visits to the Highland Folk Museum in Kingussie, Scotland, and to the Museum of English Rural Life (now the Rural History Centre) in Reading, England, produced photographs from their collections. Swedish basket-stories came from Karin Lundholm, Järvsö; and Jonas Hasselrot, Sodertalje. In Germany, I owe thanks to Michael Thierschmann, Mengsberg.

INSTITUTIONS VISITED

From 1999–2002, my husband Don and I searched most Acadian collections in Atlantic Canada, and some related collections beyond our shores.

NOVA SCOTIA
History Collection, Nova Scotia Museum, Halifax
Nova Scotia Archives and Records Management, Halifax
Killam Memorial Library, Dalhousie University
Archelaus Smith Museum, Clark's Harbour
Musée Acadien de Pubnico-Ouest, West Pubnico
Yarmouth County Museum, Yarmouth
La Vieille Maison, Meteghan
Centre Acadien, Université Sainte-Anne, Church Point
Wallace Area Museum, Wallace
Sunrise Trail Museum, Tatamagouche
The Acadian House Museum, Chezzetcook
Nicolas Denys Museum, St. Peters
Fortress Louisbourg, Louisbourg
North Highlands Community Museum, Dingwall
Les Trois Pignons, Chéticamp
Acadian Museum, Chéticamp
Margaree Bicentennial Museum, Margaree

PRINCE EDWARD ISLAND
Musée Acadien, Miscouche
Alberton Museum, Alberton
Village de l'Acadie, Mont Carmel
Orwell Corner Museum, Orwell Corner
The Cultural Centre, Summerside

NEW BRUNSWICK
Musée Acadien, University of Moncton
Centre for Acadian Studies, University of Moncton
Musée Acadien, Caraquet
Village Historique Acadien, Caraquet
Musée Historique de Madawaska, Edmunston

NEWFOUNDLAND AND LABRADOR
Provincial Museum of Newfoundland and Labrador, St. John's
Craft Council of Newfoundland and Labrador, St. John's
Fédération des Francophones de Terre-Neuve et du Labrador, St. John's
Provincial Archives of Newfoundland and Labrador, St. John's
Memorial University, Folklore Archives and Centre for Newfoundland Studies, St. John's
Kendall Library, Gilbert Higgens Collection, Stephenville
Cornerbrook Museum and Archives, Cornerbrook
Cercle des Mémoires Musée, Port-au-Port
Old Priest's House Museum, Port-au-Port

QUÉBEC
Canadian Museum of Civilization, Gatineau
Musée de la Civilisation, Québec
Musée de l'Amérique Française, Québec
Musée des Augustines, Québec
Musée des Ursulines, Québec
McCord Museum, Montréal
Gespeg, Fontenelle
Musée de la Gaspésie, Gaspé
Musée Acadien du Québec, Bonaventure
Micmac Cooperative, Maria

UNITED STATES
New York State Office of Parks, Recreation and Historic Preservation, Waterford, NY

Bibliography

PUBLISHED MATERIAL

Ågren, Katarina and Karin Lundholm. *Näverslöjd*. 2nd ed. Västerås [Sweden]: ICA Bokförlag, 1976.

Anger, Dorothy. "Traces: Traditional Material Culture of the Newfoundland Micmac." Final Project Summary. March 1983. Provincial Museum of Newfoundland and Labrador, St. John's, NL.

Arsenault, Bona. *History of the Acadians*. Ottawa: Leméac, 1978.

Barratt, Mary. *Oak Swill Basket-Making in the Lake District*. Cumbria, UK: n.p., 1983.

"Basket Making—Reviving an Old Tradition." *Miawputek Aqnutemakn*, Vol. 1, No.4, 1996:3, Conne River, NL.

Brettell, Richard R., Karen Zukowski, and Joachim Pissarro. *Camille Pissarro in the Caribbean, 1850–1855: Drawings from the Collection at Olana*. St. Thomas, Virgin Islands: Hebrew Congregation of St. Thomas, 1996.

Butcher, Mary. "Basketmaking in Poland." *Basketmakers' Association Newsletter* [UK]. No. 59 (1991): 11-32.

Butcher, Mary. *Contemporary International Basketmaking*. London, UK: Merrell Holberton, 1999.

Cormier, Yves. *Dictionnaire de Français Acadien*. Québec, QC: Fides, 1999.

Cozzens, Frederic S. *Acadia; or A Month with the Blue Noses*. 2nd ed. Cambridge: Riverside, 1877.

Creasey, John S. *Victorian and Edwardian Country Life from Old Photographs*. London: B.T. Batsford, 1977.

Davies, D. J. "A Lifelong Affair with Willow." *Basketmakers' Association Newsletter* [UK]. No. 88 (1999): 5-8.

Delvaux, Edmond M. "La Vannerie en Coudrier à Silenrieux." *Enquêtes du Musée de la Vie Wallonne* [Belgium]. III, 32-33 (1934-1935): 227-244.

Duchesne, R., H. Ferrand, and J. Thomas. *La Vannerie: L'Osier*. Paris [France]: Baillière, 1981.

Dupont, Jean-Claude. *Histoire Populaire de l'Acadie*. Ottawa: Leméac, 1978.

Eaton, Allen H. *Handicrafts of the Southern Highlands* [USA]. New York: Dover, 1973.

Etienne-Nugue, Jocelyn. *Artisanats Traditionnels en Afrique Noire: Burkina Faso*. Dakar, Institut Culturel Africain, 1982.

Etienne-Nugue, Jocelyn. *Artisanats Traditionnels en Afrique Noire: Côte d'Ivorie*. Dakar, Institut Culturel Africain, 1985.

Etienne-Nugue, Jocelyn. *Artisanats Traditionnels en Afrique Noire: Bénin*. Dakar, Institut Culturel Africain, 1987.

Etienne-Nugue, Jocelyn. *Artisanats Traditionnels en Afrique Noire: Niger*. Dakar, Institut Culturel Africain, 1990.

Ferguson, Leland. *Uncommon Ground: Archaeology and Early America, 1650–1800*. Washington, DC: Smithsonian, 1992.

Fitzgerald, Alison. "A Ciseog." *Basketmakers' Association Newsletter* [UK]. 40 (1986): 6-9.

Fitzgerald, Alison. "When is a Ciseog not a Ciseog?...When it's a Sciathog!" *Basketmakers' Association Newsletter* [UK]. 41 (1987): 13-14.

Fitzgibbon, Theodora. *A Taste of Scotland: Scottish Traditional Food with Period Photographs Specifically Prepared by George Morrison*. New York: Avenal Books, 1970.

Fuller, Steve. "Cumberland Swills." *Basketmakers' Association Newsletter* [UK]. 85 (1998): 39-41.

Gabriel, Sue and Sally Goymer. *The Complete Book of Basketry Techniques*. Newton Abbott, UK: David and Charles, 1991.

Gordon, Joleen. *Edith Clayton's Market Basket: A Heritage of Splintwood Basketry in Nova Scotia*. Halifax: Nova Scotia Museum, 1977.

Gordon, Joleen. *Handwoven Hats: A History of Straw, Wood and Rush Hats in Nova Scotia*. Halifax: Nova Scotia Museum, 1981.

Gordon, Joleen. *Withe Baskets, Traps and Brooms: Traditional Crafts in Nova Scotia*. Halifax: Nova Scotia Museum, 1984.

Gordon, Joleen. "Micmac Indian Basketry." *The Art of Native American Basketry: a Living Legacy*. Ed. Frank W. Porter. Westport, CT: Greenwood, 1990: 17-44.

Gordon, Joleen. *Construction and Reconstruction of a Mi'kmaq Sixteenth Century Cedar-Bark Bag*. Curatorial Report No. 76. Halifax: Nova Scotia Museum, 1993.

Gordon, Joleen. *Mi'kmaq Textiles: Sewn-Cattail Matting, BkCp-1 Site, Pictou, Nova Scotia*. Curatorial Report No. 80. Halifax: Nova Scotia Museum, 1995.

Gordon, Joleen. *Mi'kmaq Textiles: Twining: Rush and Other Fibres, BkCp-1 Site, Pictou, Nova Scotia*. Curatorial Report No. 82. Halifax: Nova Scotia Museum, 1997.

Grant, I. F. *Highland Folk Ways*. London, UK: Routledge and Kegan Paul, 1961.

Griffiths, Naomi E. S. "The Acadians of Belle-Ile-en-Mer." *Natural History*. 90. 1 (1981a): 48-56.

Griffiths, Naomi E. S. "The Acadians who had a problem in France." *Canadian Geographic*. 101. 4. (1981b): 40-45.

Guth, Ann. *The Baskets of St. John, US Virgin Islands*. n.p., 1982.

Hasselrot, Jonas. *Korgar: Tradition och Teknik*. Stockholm, [Sweden]: LTs Förlag, 1997.

Hasselrot, Jonas. "Rib Baskets in Sweden." *Basketmakers' Association Newsletter* [UK]. 86 (1998): 12-15.

Hogan, Joe. *Basketmaking in Ireland*. Wicklow, [Ireland]: Wordwell, 2001.

Innes, Fran. "A Tisket, A Tasket, I Found a Yellow Basket." *Decks Awash*. 8. 4 (1979): 60-61.

Irwin, John Rice. *Baskets and Basketmakers in Southern Appalachia*. Exton, PA: Schiffer, 1982.

Kemp, Bernard. "Basketmaking on the Island of St. John." *The Clarion*. 15. 3 (1990): 52-59.

Law, Rachel Nash and Cynthia W. Taylor. *Appalachian White Oak Basketmaking: Handing Down the Basket*. Knoxville: University of Tennessee Press, 1991.

Lebreton, Clarence. *Hier l'Acadie, Scenes du Village Historique Acadien*. Barcelona, [Spain]: Editorial Escudo de Oro, 1981.

Lescarbot, Marc. *Nova Francia (Histoire de la Nouvelle France, 1609)*. Trans. P. Erondelle. 2nd ed. London, UK: Harper, 1928.

Lynch, Colleen. *Crafts of Newfoundland and Labrador*. St. John's, NL: Department of Rural Development, Newfoundland and Labrador, 1979.

Mackley, Florence M. *Handweaving in Cape Breton*. Sydney, NS: 2nd ed. n.p., 1977.

Marshall, Ingeborg. *A History and Ethnography of the Beothuk*. Montreal and Kingston: McGill-Queen's University Press, 1996.

Matthews, Ralph. "There's No Better Place than Here": *Social Change in Three Newfoundland Communities*. Book Society of Canada, 1976.

McGhee, Robert. *Ancient People of the Arctic*. Vancouver: UBC Press and Canadian Museum of Civilization, 1996.

Morris, Vanessa and Hugh Cheape. "Creels and Skulls: Form and Function." *Scotland's Crafts*. Ed. Louise Butler. Edinburgh: NMS, 2000:85-100.

National Archives Census Records, 1714.

"Nécrologie," *L'Évangéline*. Weymouth, Digby County, NS, 24 September 1891: 3.

Oldendorp, C. G. A. *History of the Mission of the Evangelical Brethren on the Caribbean Islands of St. Thomas, St. Croix and St. John*. Ed. Johann Jakob Bossard/Trans. Arnold R. Highfield and Valdimir Barac. Ann Arbor, MI: Karoma, 1987.

Paul, Frances. *Spruce Root Basketry of the Alaska Tlingit*. Sitka, Alaska: 2nd ed. Friends of the Sheldon Jackson Museum, 1991.

Perry, Hattie A. *Old Days Old Ways: Early 20th century Nova Scotia*. Tantallon, NS: Four East, 1989.

Shaw-Smith, David. *Ireland's Traditional Crafts*. London, UK: Thames and Hudson, 1984.

Stephenson, Sue H. *Basketry of the Appalachian Mountains*. New York: Van Nostrand Reinhold, 1977.

Stewart, Hilary. *Cedar: Tree of Life to the Northwest Coast Indians*. Vancouver: Douglas and McIntyre, 1984.

Thibodeau, Félix E. *Le Parler de la Baie Sainte-Marie*. Yarmouth, NS: Lescarbot, 1988.

Thierschmann, Michael. *Selber Flechten Lernen, ein Lehrgang in die Welt des Korbflechtens*. Kandern, Germany: Werksiedlung Sankt Christoph, 1996.

Thompson, Francis. *Victorian and Edwardian Highlands from Old Photographs*. London: B.T. Batsford, 1976.

Vaughan, Betty Boudreau. *I'll Buy You an Ox*. Halifax: Nimbus, 1997.

Verdet-Fierz, Bernard and Regula. *Willow Basketry*. Loveland, CO: Interweave, 1993. Trans. of Anleitung zum Flechten mit Weiden. Trans. W. Smith. Switzerland: Paul Haupt, 1993.

Wallace, Birgitta. "L'Anse aux Meadows. Gateway to Vinland." *Acta Archaeologica*. 61. (1991): 166-197.

Wallis, W.D. and R. S. Wallis. *The Micmac Indians of Eastern Canada*. Minneapolis: University of Minnesota Press, 1955.

Whitehead, Ruth Holmes. *Elitekey, Micmac Material Culture from 1600 A.D. to the Present*. Halifax: Nova Scotia Museum, 1980.

Whitehead, Ruth Holmes. *Micmac Quillwork: Micmac Indian Techniques of Porcupine Quill Decoration, 1600–1950*. Halifax: Nova Scotia Museum, 1982.

Whitehead, Ruth Holmes. *Plant Fibre Textiles from the Hopps Site: BkCp-1*. Curatorial Report No. 59. Halifax: Nova Scotia Museum, [1986].

Whitehead, Ruth Holmes. "I Have Lived Here Since the World Began: Atlantic Coast Artistic Traditions." *The Spirit Sings: Artistic Traditions of Canada's First Peoples*. Toronto: McClelland and Stewart and the Glenbow Museum, 1987. 17-50.

Wright, Dorothy. *The Complete Book of Baskets and Basketry*. 2nd ed. Newton Abbot, UK: David and Charles, 1983.

UNPUBLISHED MATERIAL

Anonymous. "Carpe Diem: Tempus Fugit." Student Oral History Project, 2 vols. Stephenville, NL: Kindale Library, 1978.

Nova Scotia Museum Library, Halifax. "Harry Pier Papers. Mi'kmaw Ethnology Notes." Translated, edited and annotated by Ruth Holmes Whitehead, 2003.

Pelletier, Gaby. "The Analysis and Classification of Maliseet Splint Ash Baskets." Senior study. Fredericton, University of New Brunswick, 1973.